JOHN C. CALHOUN

AND THE ROOTS OF WAR

THE HISTORY OF THE CIVIL WAR

CLARA BARTON: *Healing the Wounds*

JOHN C. CALHOUN *and the Roots of War*

JOHN ERICSSON *and the Inventions of War*

DAVID FARRAGUT *and the Great Naval Blockade*

ULYSSES S. GRANT *and the Strategy of Victory*

STONEWALL JACKSON: *Lee's Greatest Lieutenant*

ANDREW JOHNSON: *Rebuilding the Union*

ROBERT E. LEE *and the Rise of the South*

ABRAHAM LINCOLN: *To Preserve the Union*

HARRIET TUBMAN: *Slavery and the Underground Railroad*

THE HISTORY OF THE CIVIL WAR

JOHN C. CALHOUN

AND THE ROOTS OF WAR

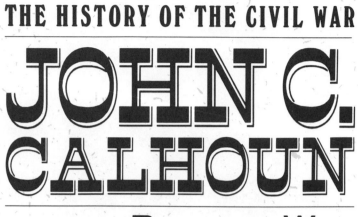

by **TERESA CELSI**

INTRODUCTORY ESSAY BY
HENRY STEELE COMMAGER

SILVER BURDETT PRESS

Series Editorial Supervisor: Richard G. Gallin
Series Editing: Agincourt Press
Series Consultant: Leah Fortson
Cover and Text Design: Circa 86, Inc.
Series Supervision of Art and Design: Leslie Bauman
Maps: Susan Johnston Carlson

Consultants: Rudy Johnson, Social Studies Coordinator, Lansing
Public Schools, Lansing, Michigan; Arnold Markoe, Professor,
Brooklyn College, City University of New York.

Library of Congress Cataloging-in-Publication Data
Celsi, Teresa Noel.
    John C. Calhoun and the roots of war / by Teresa Celsi :
introduction by Henry Steele Commager.
      p.   cm. — (The History of the Civil War)
    Includes bibliographical references.
    Includes index.
    Summary: A biography of the senator from South Carolina who fought
for the South's interests and to keep the institution of slavery.
    1. Calhoun, John C. (John Caldwell), 1782–1850—Juvenile
literature.   2. Legislators—United States—Biography—Juvenile
literature.   3. United States. Congress. Senate—Biography—
Juvenile literature.   4. United States—Politics and
government—1783–1865—Juvenile literature.   [1. Calhoun, John C.
(John Caldwell), 1782–1850.   2. Statesmen.   3. United States—
Politics and government—1783–1865.]   I. Title.   II. Series.
    E340.C15C43   1991
    973.5′092—dc20
    [B]
    [92]   90-20067
    ISBN 0-382-24045-6 (pbk) : ISBN 0-382-09936-2 (lib. bdg.)   CIP
                                                                  AC

TABLE OF CONTENTS

Introduction by Henry Steele Commager   6

Civil War Time Line   8

Chapter 1   Long Cane Creek   13

        2   New Haven, Charleston, and Litchfield   22

        3   The *Chesapeake* Affair   31

        4   The War of 1812   40

        5   Hartford, New Orleans, and Ghent   47

        6   Building a Nation   54

        7   The War Department   61

        8   The Missouri Compromise   68

        9   Elections and Politics   75

       10   John Calhoun and Andrew Jackson   82

       11   The Nullification Crisis   88

       12   Slavery   96

       13   Texas and Oregon   103

       14   Inventions and Progress   110

       15   The Compromise of 1850   118

Timetable of Events in the Life of John C. Calhoun   128

Suggested Reading   129

Selected Sources   130

Index   131

Senator, vice-president, and presidential candidate, John C. Calhoun of South Carolina is a difficult historical character to understand. During the whole of his mature life he was in the public eye, but he kept very much to himself. An ardent patriot of his state, to whose interests and welfare he pledged his whole life, he nevertheless chose New England for his education. He graduated from Yale College, and then studied law at the Litchfield Law School in Connecticut. He then returned to South Carolina and threw himself at once into politics. He was elected to the state legislature and then to the United States Congress, to which he devoted the next 40 years of his life.

Calhoun was at first an ardent champion of a strong national government. Much of his life was committed to work in the Senate, and he eventually became vice-president. He had little influence in that role, however. Later, as secretary of war under President Monroe and secretary of state under President Tyler, he proved to be the most experienced statesman of his generation.

But there was a drawback to Calhoun's politics—a serious, perhaps even fatal flaw. In his later political life, Calhoun saw himself not as a representative of his state or of his political party, but rather took on the role of spokesman for the entire South. What that meant in Calhoun's day was being a spokesman for slavery. And slavery was under attack. The attack grew more and more bitter, more and more uncompromising, as Calhoun lent himself more to the defense of that institution. In that defense, Calhoun developed what came to be known as the "proslavery argument."

It was an argument based on a complex situation. Slavery was a necessity, the argument said. It could not be avoided. Slavery was a blessing for whites and blacks. It was good for whites, said Calhoun, because it gave them time to develop their own culture. It relieved them of the burden of tending their crops or doing other work. For the slaves, Calhoun claimed slavery to be a many-sided blessing. They had been snatched from Africa where they were subject to war and starvation. They were given the "benefits" of civilization, were clothed and fed and, most importantly, were made into Christians.

Calhoun's argument was not popular with everyone, especially in the North. Though it salved the conscience of slavery supporters, it angered people such as William Lloyd Garrison and Theodore Parker. These men, and others like them, were abolitionists—people who believed in eliminating slavery and were beginning to do something about it.

Europe also reacted negatively to Calhoun's support of the "peculiar institution," as England's Lord Chancellor, Lord Mansfield, called slavery. Earlier, Mansfield had swept that institution aside in his country with the words "England is too pure an air for slaves to breathe in."

Ten years after the aged Calhoun listened to a reading of his last speech in the Senate—a speech still defending slavery—John Brown, a radical abolitionist, went to the gallows for "treason against the state of Virginia." He had tried to use militant means to end slavery, and was being hanged for his attempt. As he went to his death, he murmured his last words: "Today I am the most valuable man in America."

In a few short years the American Civil War would begin. Though he had been dead for over a decade, John C. Calhoun had had a role in the beginning of that war, and in shaping the course of American history for years to come.

CIVIL WAR TIME LINE

May 22
Kansas-Nebraska Act states that in new territories the question of slavery will be decided by the citizens. Many Northerners are outraged because this act could lead to the extension of slavery.

| 1854 | 1855 | 1856 | 1857 |

May 21
Lawrence, Kansas is sacked by proslavery Missourians.

May 22
Senator Charles Sumner is caned by Preston Brooks for delivering a speech against slavery.

May 24 – 25
Pottawatomie Creek massacre committed by John Brown and four of his sons.

March 6
The Supreme Court, in the *Dred Scott* ruling, declares that blacks are not U. S. citizens, and therefore cannot bring lawsuits. The ruling divides the country on the question of the legal status of blacks.

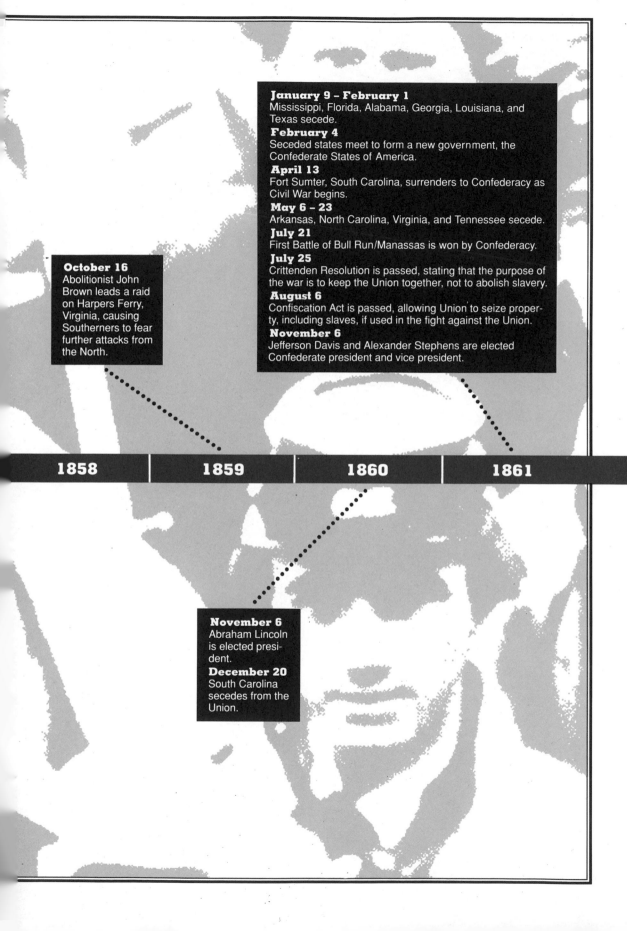

January 9 – February 1
Mississippi, Florida, Alabama, Georgia, Louisiana, and Texas secede.

February 4
Seceded states meet to form a new government, the Confederate States of America.

April 13
Fort Sumter, South Carolina, surrenders to Confederacy as Civil War begins.

May 6 – 23
Arkansas, North Carolina, Virginia, and Tennessee secede.

July 21
First Battle of Bull Run/Manassas is won by Confederacy.

July 25
Crittenden Resolution is passed, stating that the purpose of the war is to keep the Union together, not to abolish slavery.

August 6
Confiscation Act is passed, allowing Union to seize property, including slaves, if used in the fight against the Union.

November 6
Jefferson Davis and Alexander Stephens are elected Confederate president and vice president.

October 16
Abolitionist John Brown leads a raid on Harpers Ferry, Virginia, causing Southerners to fear further attacks from the North.

1858	1859	1860	1861

November 6
Abraham Lincoln is elected president.

December 20
South Carolina secedes from the Union.

February 6
Fort Henry, Tennessee, is captured.
February 16
Fort Donelson, Tennessee, is captured by Union.
March 9
Monitor and *Merrimack* battle near Hampton Roads, Virginia.
March 23
Shenandoah Valley Campaign opens with Union victory over Maj. Gen. Thomas J. "Stonewall" Jackson.
April 7
Gen. Ulysses S. Grant wins Battle of Shiloh, Tennessee, splitting rebel forces on the Mississippi River.
April 25
New Orleans is captured by Union naval forces led by flag officer David Farragut.
June 19
Slavery is abolished in U. S. territories.
June 25
Gen. Robert E. Lee leads rout of Gen. George McClellan's army in the Seven Days Battles.
July 17
The United States Congress authorizes formation of the first black regiments.
August 29 – 30
Second Battle of Bull Run/Manassas is won by Confederacy.
September 5
Lee leads first Confederate invasion of the North into Maryland.
September 17
Battle of Antietam/Sharpsburg, bloodiest of the war, ends in a stalemate between Lee and McClellan.

1862   **1863**   **1864**   **1865**

January 1
Lincoln issues Emancipation Proclamation, freeing slaves in Confederate states.
March 3
U.S. Congress passes its first military draft.
April 2
Bread riots occur in Richmond, Virginia.
May 1 – 4
Battle of Chancellorsville is won by Confederacy; Stonewall Jackson is accidentally shot by his own troops.
May 22 – July 4
Union wins siege of Vicksburg in Mississippi.
June 3
Lee invades the North from Fredericksburg, Virginia.
July 3
Battle of Gettysburg is won in Pennsylvania by Union.
July 13 – 17
Riots occur in New York City over the draft.
November 19
Lincoln delivers the Gettysburg Address.

March 12
Grant becomes general-in-chief of Union army.
May 5 – 6
Lee and Lt. Gen. James Longstreet defeat Grant at the Wilderness Battle in Virginia.
May 6 – September 2
Atlanta Campaign ends in Union general William Tecumseh Sherman's occupation of Atlanta.
May 8 – 19
Lee and Grant maneuver for position in the Spotsylvania Campaign.
June 3
Grant is repelled at Cold Harbor, Virginia.
June 18, 1864 – April 2, 1865
Grant conducts the Siege of Petersburg, in Virginia, ending with evacuation of the city and Confederate withdrawal from Richmond.
August 5
Admiral Farragut wins Battle of Mobile Bay for Union.
October 6
Union general Philip Sheridan lays waste to Shenandoah Valley, Virginia, cutting off Confederacy's food supplies.
November 8
Lincoln is reelected president.
November 15 – December 13
Sherman's March to the Sea ends with Union occupation of Savannah, Georgia.

March 2
First Reconstruction Act is passed, reorganizing governments of Southern states.

| **1866** | **1867** | **1868** | **1869** |

April 9
Civil Rights Act of 1866 is passed. Among other things, it removes states' power to keep former slaves from testifying in court or owning property.

November 3
Ulysses S. Grant is elected president.

January 31
Thirteenth Amendment, freeing slaves, is passed by Congress and sent to states for ratification.
February 1 – April 26
Sherman invades the Carolinas.
February 6
Lee is appointed general-in-chief of Confederate armies.
March 3
Freedman's Bureau is established to assist former slaves.
April 9
Lee surrenders to Grant at Appomattox Courthouse, Virginia.
April 15
Lincoln dies from assassin's bullet; Andrew Johnson becomes president.
May 26
Remaining Confederate troops surrender.

LONG CANE CREEK

"We worked in the field and many's the times in the brilin' sun me and Marse John has plowed together."

SAWNEY, A SLAVE IN THE
CALHOUN HOUSEHOLD

One day in the late 1790s, a neighbor came upon John Caldwell Calhoun and found the young farmer plowing a field. There was nothing unusual about that. Most of the land in this part of South Carolina—known as the Long Cane Creek settlement—was farmland, and the sight of a young man plowing was common. What made the scene unusual was that attached to the plow, tied on with a bit of rope, was a book. While he was busy working, Calhoun was also reading.

At the time, John Calhoun was in his late teens, but he had been running the Calhoun household for several years. His father, Patrick, had died when John was almost 14.

Patrick Calhoun had arrived in North America as a child. His family was Scotch-Irish and had settled, as most of the Scotch-Irish did, along the frontier. The frontier had plenty of land for them to clear, build their houses on, and farm. In Europe, all the land had been taken for centuries, but here they could have their own farms. It was a great opportunity.

But life on the frontier was very dangerous. As more and more Europeans came to North America, the frontier was pushed farther and farther into Native American territory. The frontier was on the western edge of the European colonies in North America, and Native American tribes in the area did not want more settlers on their land. Usually the Native Americans were not paid for the land that the Europeans settled on. Many Native Americans fought back, killing the settlers. Settlers on the frontier did not have the protection that could be offered to colonists nearer the coast.

In 1755, the area where Patrick Calhoun and his family lived was in danger of attack by the Six Nations, a group of Native American tribes. Calhoun learned of another area, the Long Cane Creek district (known officially as the District of 96). It was far enough away so that the Six Nations would not bother them. The principal tribe in the District of 96 was the Cherokee, who were friendly to settlers. Calhoun led his neighbors to this new area. They started to build their homes and organize a church.

For a few years, everything was fine. But the Cherokee came to resent Calhoun and the others. In 1760, they attacked the settlement. Among the settlers killed in the attack were Patrick Calhoun's mother and brother.

The settlers needed protection. Calhoun made the long journey to the capital in Columbia to speak to the government, which was called the Provincial Assembly. He asked for help in patrolling the District of 96, building roads, and setting up a court to try criminals. The Provincial Assembly was composed of people from the coastal plains. They did not care about the "up-country," as the frontier was known, and they refused to help.

Patrick Calhoun and his neighbors decided to take their defense into their own hands. They created a company of rangers to patrol the area. Calhoun served as the captain. But the settlers resented the Provincial Assembly for not helping them. They paid the same taxes that everyone paid, but they had effectively no representation in the assembly, and their needs were not being met. Finally, the Long Cane settlers took action. In 1769, they marched down to the capital in a body and elected Patrick Calhoun to the legislature. Even then, after traveling 200 miles, Calhoun's men were forced to defend themselves with guns while casting their ballots.

The next year, Calhoun married Martha Caldwell, a tall, dark woman from the Long Cane settlement. Her family had come with Calhoun when they first settled the area, 14 years earlier. She was not only beautiful, but intelligent and studious, too. Her skills as a manager were invaluable to Patrick Calhoun. He needed her to run his farms while he was away serving in the legislature.

In 1776, the Revolutionary War swept through South Carolina, and Charleston fought off an attack by the British army. Martha Calhoun's brother, John Caldwell, was a major in the Continental Army. He was killed by the British, and his house was burned to the ground.

When Martha and Patrick Calhoun's fourth child was born, they named him John Caldwell Calhoun in memory of Martha's brother. The war was still raging, but in the year John was born, George Washington defeated British General Sir Charles Cornwallis at Yorktown. Before John was a year old, the war ended.

Highlights in the Life of John C. Calhoun

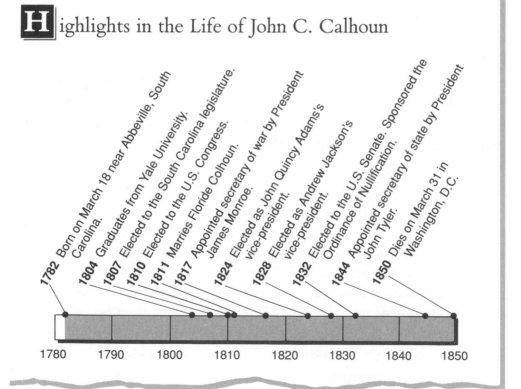

After the Revolutionary War was over, the United States began to work together as a nation—but it was an uneasy transition from the colonial days. The 13 colonies had originally been settled by very different people. Many had come to the country to start religious communities. The Puritans had settled in New England. Maryland was a Catholic community. Pennsylvania had been settled by Quakers, who invited other sects to join them. The Southern states were populated mainly with Episcopalians. Besides the religious differences, there were economic differences. People in the New England states made money by trading, fishing, and shipbuilding. They were just starting to build factories. The Southern states used their broad, fertile land and warm climate to produce raw materials, mostly tobacco and rice. After the revolution, more and more planters in the South started growing cotton, too.

Some of the colonies had existed for more than 150 years. For much of that time, it was extremely difficult to travel from one colony to another. The distances were great, and there were few roads. In some cases, it was actually easier to travel from a colony to Europe than from one colony to another. This distance between colonies increased the differences between their inhabitants.

For the first few years, the states relied on the Articles of Confederation to run the country. This document created the Continental Congress. In the Congress, each state had one vote. But people were not happy with the Confederation. They wanted a stronger government.

In 1787, delegates from the 13 states attended a Constitutional Convention in Philadelphia. General George Washington himself acted as president. One of the objectives of the convention was to write a constitution. But some crucial issues had to be resolved before this could be done.

The first issue to be settled was a dispute between the states with small populations and the states with many people. The large states felt that having more people entitled them to more political power. They thought that representatives to Congress should be chosen according to population—one representative for a given number of people. By this method, a heavily populated state such as Virginia would have many more votes than a small state such as Delaware. The small states thought that the government should continue to operate as it had under the Articles of Confederation, with each state having one vote, regardless of population.

The delegates to the convention came up with a compromise. The Constitution created a Congress divided into two houses, the House of Representatives and the Senate. Representatives were chosen by population, and larger states would have more representatives than small states. But the Senate would not be based on population. States would choose two senators, so that in the Senate, each state would have the same number of votes, no matter what its size.

Slavery was another issue that had to be faced in setting up a common government. Because slaves made up such a large part of the Southern population, states in this region wanted to count each slave as a person when electing representatives. This was despite the fact that the slaves were not allowed to vote. The Northerners objected. They felt it was unreasonable to include slaves in the population count because slaves were not really represented politically. Besides, there were not many slaves in the North. The Southern states would have more representatives than the Northern states if the slaves were counted the same as free men. The states compromised by counting a slave as three-fifths of a free person.

There were some people in the North who wanted to ban the slave trade completely. They felt that slavery was immoral. In a nation that declared in its own constitution that "all men are created equal," it seemed wrong that people could be treated differently because of the color of their skin.

But slavery was vitally important to the South. Large plantations required the labor of many people, but few workers were available to do that labor for a low enough wage. Though many Northerners objected to slavery, the need to bring the colonies together into a nation was more important to them than the moral drawbacks of slavery. Another compromise was reached, and the slave trade was allowed to continue until 1808.

The delegates drafted a constitution, but a problem arose when it was presented to the states for ratification. There was nothing in it to protect the rights of individual citizens. This disturbed Thomas Jefferson, the author of the Declaration of Independence. He could see a time when a majority of people could use their power to oppress a minority. He wrote to his friend James Madison, who had worked on the Constitution, and suggested adding a Bill of Rights to protect individuals.

Madison saw the wisdom of this proposal, and he pushed to add the Bill of Rights in a series of amendments. Amendments are additions to a contract. An amendment could be added to the Constitution if at least two-thirds of the states voted for it. Because of Madison's proposal, many states that were hesitating decided to adopt the new Constitution. South Carolina became the eighth state to ratify the Constitution on May 23, 1788.

At that time, John Calhoun was six years old. His life was simple, full of the everyday duties of a planter's son. He now had a

younger brother, named Patrick after their father. The Calhouns grew all their own fruits and vegetables on their five farms, and they also planted cotton to sell. John and little Patrick had to pick out an ounce of cotton seeds from the cotton fibers every day. An ounce is only about a handful, but cotton seeds are tiny, and it was difficult work.

After that, and their other chores, John and his brother were free to enjoy themselves. John was fond of fishing and shooting. He would also spend hours sitting quietly on the edge of the creek with his playmate Sawney. Sawney was the son of the first slave whom Patrick Calhoun had ever owned. By now, the Calhouns had 30 slaves, but John felt closest to Sawney.

John was probably taught to read by his mother. There was no school within a hundred miles of the Calhouns' home. But there were a few books. Every home had a Bible, and when he was 13, John had read Thomas Paine's *The Rights of Man* enough times to memorize passages from it.

At night, John would listen to his parents talk about the issues of the day. Patrick Calhoun was not pleased with the new Constitution. South Carolina had a tradition of fighting for its independence. During the Revolutionary War, the state had fought 137 battles with the British forces. South Carolina was proud of its liberty. To Patrick Calhoun, the Constitution was simply another threat to South Carolina's independence.

When John was 13, a traveling preacher came to stay at their house. His name was Moses Waddel. The Calhouns did not know him, but they could see he was educated and well-bred, and they welcomed him into their home.

Moses Waddel was struck by the beauty of John's older sister, Catherine. He asked her to marry him, and she agreed. Waddel took Catherine to his home in Columbia County, Georgia, where he opened up a school. John Calhoun went with them and became one of Waddel's students.

Within a year of their marriage, Catherine died. Waddel was heartbroken. He could not bring himself to continue the school, so he closed it. Then he tried to forget his loss by traveling as a preacher again.

When Waddel closed the school and left, Calhoun stayed behind. For more than three months, he was practically alone in the house, with only Waddel's library to keep him company. Those three months changed Calhoun's life.

As a preacher, Waddel had, of course, many books on religion, but John Calhoun had never been interested in the subject. He turned his attention to the history books. Suddenly, a whole new world opened up—a world of heroes and battles, explorers and statesmen. Calhoun read ancient history, including the story of Rome and how it grew from a small republic to a vast empire. He read about the history of America and the voyages of Captain Cook. He was so excited that he sometimes forgot to eat or sleep. By the time Waddel returned, Calhoun had made himself sick. Alarmed, Waddel sent Calhoun home.

When Calhoun arrived home, there was more bad news. Patrick Calhoun had died while John was in Georgia. At 14, John was the oldest male Calhoun still at home. His older brothers, William and James, had left to start their careers as tradesmen. The responsibility for running the farms fell on John and his mother.

Martha Caldwell Calhoun was an excellent manager. John could not have had a better partner. For the next five years, they kept the farms running at a profit. But it took more than planning and organizing to run the farms. It took backbreaking labor, too. Calhoun himself plowed the fields, while Sawney followed behind, dropping the precious cotton seeds two or three at a time into the furrows.

The work took all day, and there was little time during the sunlight hours for the luxury of reading. That was how Calhoun came up with the idea of tying a book to his plow. With his shoulder to the plow handle, and his head bowed under the fierce sun, Calhoun could a least snatch a few sentences at a time.

It soon became obvious to the residents of Long Cane Creek that Calhoun's talents were being wasted on the farm. The neighbors started urging Martha to have him continue his education.

But Calhoun would not hear of it. He had been born a planter, and his life was the farms. Although reading gave him great pleasure, his main responsibility was to the land his family owned. Like his book, John Caldwell Calhoun was tied to the plow.

NEW HAVEN, CHARLESTON, AND LITCHFIELD

"I have so much confidence in the good sense of
man, and his qualifications for self-government
that I am never afraid of the issue where reason is
left free to exert her force. . . . "

THOMAS JEFFERSON

"Why was government instituted at all? Because
the passions of men will not conform to the
dictates of reason and justice without restraint."

ALEXANDER HAMILTON

While John Calhoun was busy on his farm, President George Washington was finishing his second term. Washington's leadership was very important to the country. Actually, running a nation as a republic was a bold new experiment. The Greeks had invented the idea of democracy, or government by the people, thousands of years before. The Romans then based their notion of a republic, or representative government, on this Greek ideal. But the United States was the first major experiment in democratic government in the modern world. Many people were not sure it would work.

But having George Washington as president helped. Washington was not just admired by the people of the United States—he was loved. If anyone could make the new government work, Americans felt, it would be him.

Washington tried to be fair in setting up his cabinet. He picked people from all parts of the country. He chose Thomas Jefferson, from Virginia, to be secretary of state and Alexander Hamilton, from New York, as secretary of the treasury.

Thomas Jefferson, framer of the Declaration of Independence and third president of the United States.

Jefferson and Hamilton often disagreed over how the new government should work. Jefferson had traveled to Europe, and he did not like what he saw. Many people in Europe were poor, hungry, and sickly. He wrote, "I find the general fate of humanity here. The truth of Voltaire's observation offers itself perpetually, that every man here must be either the hammer or the anvil." He blamed the situation on greedy rulers who had oppressed the people for centuries. Left to themselves, he believed, people were good. Thomas Jefferson saw in the United States a chance for a new beginning—a place where people could develop freely.

Alexander Hamilton viewed things differently. Although he had fought bravely in the Revolutionary War, he was not happy with the idea of creating a new, freer type of government. He believed that people acted out of self-interest, rather than goodness. People needed limits to keep them from hurting other people. Strong laws were necessary to provide those limits.

Alexander Hamilton did not have to look far to see what can happen in a country with too much freedom. During the French Revolution in 1789, one of the rallying cries was "Liberty!" But the French Revolution turned into a reign of terror as different groups fought to gain control of the government. There was a bloodbath of political killings. The queen of France, Marie Antoinette, had her head cut off by a mob. Her head was paraded through the streets as people cheered. Hamilton was convinced that Jefferson's ideas could bring about the same situation in the United States.

When two public figures quarrel over ideas, their quarrels become part of public life. Some people agreed with Jefferson, and some with Hamilton. Those who followed Jefferson called themselves Republicans. The Federalists sided with Hamilton.

John Calhoun would have sided with Jefferson. He would be a Republican, although he probably did not realize it yet. Long Cane was so far from any city that he hardly ever heard any news about the government. Newspapers were rare. Once, he did manage to get a copy of the *South Carolina Gazette*. It had articles about the Congress, a debate on relations with France, and a speech by the president. John studied the precious copy over and over again, underlining passages with a soft pencil. He kept it all his life.

In the summer of 1800, Calhoun's older brother, James, came to visit. He had come to believe—along with Martha Calhoun—that John had too much potential to spend his life behind a plow. James Calhoun came to persuade his brother to continue his education.

At first, John insisted that he was needed on the farm. But he gradually gave in. According to historian Margaret Coit, John told his brother: "To . . . a partial education, I answer decidedly, no. But if you are willing and able to give me a complete education, I give my consent."

"What is your idea of a complete education?" James asked him.

"The best school, college, and legal education to be had in the United States," John replied.

"How long will you require for the accomplishment of such an education?" James asked, probably wondering by now what he had gotten himself into. John decided that it would take seven years, and his brother promised to support him during that time.

Moses Waddel had re-opened his school, and Calhoun began his studies there. The school was located in the woods, and classes were held out in the open in summer. In the winter, the students were required to build their own shelters, small wooden shacks. The school allowed each student to progress at his own pace. But the studies were far from easy. Calhoun studied ancient Greek and Latin by memorizing works by the classical poets Homer and Virgil. Each night he had to learn hundreds of lines.

Calhoun excelled at his studies, and within two years decided he was ready to move on. He decided to study at Yale College, in New Haven, Connecticut.

Just a few months before Calhoun left Waddel, however, a terrible thing happened. Calhoun had gone home to visit his family. His mother had been ill, but seemed to be getting better, so Calhoun returned to Waddel Academy to finish his term. When he arrived there, he was told that Martha Calhoun had died the day after he left. Calhoun was griefstricken. Both his parents had died

within a few years of each other. When he finally set out for Yale, it must have seemed that he was leaving his old life behind him forever.

At first, Calhoun was afraid that he would not be able to keep up with the other students at Yale. After all, they had studied for years at the best schools. The first day of mathematics class, Calhoun was prepared to feel lost. But the problems presented by the teacher seemed very clear. Calhoun wrote his answers down quickly. While the professor checked his work, Calhoun was surprised to see that the other students were still struggling over the problems. He had never compared himself with other students before, so he had never realized his own abilities. Calhoun was pleased to find out that his family's faith in him was not misplaced.

Calhoun made only a few friends at Yale. One of those was John Felder. Felder was a fellow Carolinian, and he was Calhoun's only rival in mathematics class. Calhoun wrote of his friend, "I find Mr. Felder a faithful and cheering companion." It probably helped that

John Felder came from South Carolina, too. It was something they had in common.

In Calhoun's second and final year at Yale, he was noticed by the president of the college, Dr. Timothy Dwight. Yale, located in New England, leaned toward Federalist policies in its teachings. Most New England states were small in population, so that region favored a strong central government—the chief aim of Federalism. The larger, more independent, agricultural states of the South preferred Jefferson's Republicanism—a system that offered them more political power. Calhoun and John Felder disagreed with the Federalists, but they usually kept quiet. So when, one day in moral philosophy class, President Dwight asked, "What is the legitimate source of power?" he was surprised to hear John Calhoun call out, "The people!"

Dr. Dwight began to debate the issue with Calhoun on the spot. The scheduled lesson was forgotten, and the class listened as Federalist teacher and Republican student faced off. They could not convince each other, but Dr. Dwight was impressed by Calhoun's abilities in debate and his use of logic to support his position. He later remarked to a friend that Calhoun had ability enough "to be President of the United States," and that he would not be "surprised to see him one day occupy the office."

Because of the brilliance of his work, Calhoun was asked to speak at the graduation ceremonies. He worked hard on the speech, but he never delivered it. Calhoun worked himself into an illness. On commencement day, he was too sick to take part in the ceremonies.

Fortunately, Calhoun had a relative nearby, Floride Colhoun (this branch of the family spelled its name with an "o"). She was the widow of one of his cousins, who was also named John. When she heard that Calhoun was ill, she immediately wrote and offered to take her young relative into her home while he recovered. Calhoun accepted the offer gratefully.

Floride Colhoun had three children. The eldest, named John Ewing for his father, was 13. A year younger than John was a daughter, named Floride for her mother. The youngest boy was

James Edward, 6. Calhoun quickly made friends with the children, listening to the boys read the Bible and helping their mother choose schools for them.

When he recovered, Calhoun left to work at a law office in Charleston, South Carolina. Charleston was a cosmopolitan city. Its seaport served the plantations of South Carolina, shipping their crops directly to Europe or to cities in New England. The streets were crowded with travelers. The air was filled with the sounds of sea chants and coach traffic. The smells ranged from coffee and bananas lying on the docks to the sweet scent of magnolia and lilac.

Calhoun hated it. He was used to a cleaner, less chaotic environment. Although not a religious man, he was put off by what he considered the immoral air of Charleston—the theaters, the saloons, the gambling houses, and the racetrack. He once wrote to Floride Colhoun after reading about a religious revival, "What a happy change to that place; which in every thing was so extremely corrupt.... Surely no people ever so much needed a reform as those in the parishes near Charleston."

Bales of cotton sit on a South Carolina dock, waiting to be loaded onto ships.

Before long, Calhoun decided to continue his studies in a less distracting place. He chose a sleepy little town in Connecticut that was home to the best law school in the country. The town was Litchfield, and the school was the Litchfield Law School, run by Judge Tapping Reeves.

When Calhoun arrived in Litchfield, his friend John Felder was already there to welcome him. Calhoun immediately wrote a letter to Floride Colhoun, complaining of a "lonesome sensation." But, he added hopefully, "by a few days' application to studies, which to me are highly interesting, I have no doubt it will be entirely removed."

John Calhoun and John Felder never did fit in socially at Litchfield. Judge Tapping Reeve was an ardent Federalist. Most of the students and townsfolk shared his views, while John Calhoun and John Felder considered themselves Republicans. They decided it was best to keep to themselves and concentrate on their studies.

But studying law did not come easily to John Calhoun now. His interest in the subject was fading, and he had to force his mind to stay on it. He wrote Floride Colhoun and to his brother Patrick, begging them to write back with news. Although he tried to bury the fact under his lawbooks, Calhoun was homesick. He decided to finish his studies as soon as possible so that he could leave.

An incident occurred while Calhoun was at Litchfield that made him even more eager to leave. A young newspaper editor, Selleck Osborne, was jailed for writing attacks on the local Federalists. Against the wishes of his teachers, Calhoun joined in a protest at the jail where the editor was being held.

Osborne had been jailed under a law known as the Sedition Act. In 1799, Congress passed two laws called the Alien Act and the Sedition Act. The Alien Act was intended to keep French immigrants from bringing the French Revolution to the United States. It gave the president power to imprison or banish foreigners.

The Sedition Act was designed to stop abuses by newspaper editors. Under this law, an editor could be tried for printing things that were not true. Unfortunately, the government, which was controlled by the Federalists, used the act to jail Republican editors. In other words, the editors who were arrested were those who disagreed with the government in power. This was a violation of the First Amendment, which protected the rights of the press.

In 1798, two states, Kentucky and Virginia, had adopted resolutions protesting the Alien and Sedition Acts. These resolutions were based on the idea that, since the Union was formed by the "compact," or agreement, of the states, the states could stop the Federal government when it overstepped its authority. The resolutions asked the other states for support, but none of them adopted any resolutions. Finally, Kentucky and Virginia settled for voicing their strong disapproval.

The Kentucky and Virginia resolutions did not succeed in stopping the Alien and Sedition Acts. But they did help Thomas Jefferson get elected in 1800. He was the first Republican president. Jefferson tried his best to follow the example set by his fellow Virginian, George Washington. In his inaugural address, Jefferson tried to bridge the gap between the political parties, saying, "We are all republicans—we are all federalists." He adopted many of the Federalists' policies, and generally strengthened the government.

But Litchfield and other cities in New England still had a hard time accepting Jefferson. Federalists were convinced that his term would end in anarchy, just as the French Revolution had. Many thought that the New England states should secede from the Union and form their own country.

Timothy Dwight, the president of Yale, and Judge Tapping Reeve, the founder of the Litchfield Law School, were two people who advocated secession by the New England states. Even though John Calhoun supported Jefferson, he could see the logic of the Federalists' arguments. Since the states had agreed to create the federal government, it followed that the states could also dissolve the government. Even after John Calhoun left school, he would take these arguments even further. But for the time being, Calhoun was aware of only one thing: He felt out of place in the Federalist North. He returned to South Carolina as soon as he could after graduating from Litchfield. As his stagecoach pulled into Charleston, John Calhoun thought he would never go north again. His home, and his heart, were in the South.

THE *CHESAPEAKE* AFFAIR

"They have entered this House with their eye on
the Presidency and mark my words, sir, we shall
have war before the end of the session."

JOHN RANDOLPH

In June 1807, the U.S.S. *Chesapeake*, a 38-gun frigate, was just rounding Cape Henry, not far from Washington, D.C. A British ship, the H.M.S. *Leopard*, came into sight and ordered the *Chesapeake* to stop. The captain of the *Leopard* wanted to come on board and conduct a search. Britain was at war with France, and many British sailors had jumped ship in the United States to avoid going into battle. The British navy had begun stopping United States ships to search for the deserters.

Captain James Barron refused, because he believed that the British had no right to board his ship. The British often used these searches as an excuse to kidnap United States sailors and force them to serve in the British navy. This practice was called impressment.

When Captain Barron refused to let the British search his ship, the *Leopard* opened fire. The British fired three times, and, as the smoke from the cannons cleared, 21 American sailors lay dead or wounded on the deck of the *Chesapeake*. Captain Barron was forced to lower his flag and allow the British to come on board. The captain of the *Leopard* seized four men and carried them off. One of the men really was a British deserter, but the three others were United States citizens.

The *Chesapeake* incident made many people in the United States angry. John Calhoun was one of those people. He helped the town government of Charleston draw up a resolution condemning the "unjust and murderous conduct of the British."

In December 1807, President Thomas Jefferson signed the Embargo Act, eliminating trade with all other countries, including Britain. Jefferson had never been a military man. He thought that cutting off trade would hurt Britain more than any military action would. He also thought the United States could survive without foreign trade. He hoped the embargo would help make the United States more independent.

But Calhoun and others like him had been fired up by the *Chesapeake* incident. They did not want an embargo; they wanted war.

The Federalists were also unhappy with Jefferson's embargo, but for different reasons. The Southern and Western states could sell their agricultural products either to Europe or to the Northern states. But the shippers of the mid-Atlantic and New England states relied on trade with other countries for their income. Since 1793, when the war between Britain and France began, the shippers of the United States had prospered. France refused to trade with Britain, and Britain had refused to have anything to do with France. But the United States traded with both countries. The American shippers picked up all the business that the other countries dropped.

Now, under the Embargo Act, the ships lay idle and rotting. Sailors were put out to work. Opponents of the embargo started spelling the word backwards, calling it the "O grab me" Act to illustrate the deathly effect it had on the shipping industry.

To make matters worse, the British parliament enacted a policy known as the Orders in Council. These orders required that British ships seize any ships headed to a port occupied by the French. The Orders in Council were in retaliation for similar orders from France. In 1806 and 1807, Emperor Napoleon Bonaparte issued two decrees, the Berlin and Milan decrees, which ordered the French

Napoleon Bonaparte, emperor of France, brought 20 years of war and destruction to the European continent.

navy to stop any ship headed for a British port.

Responding to these events and to opposition at home, in 1809 Jefferson got Congress to repeal the Embargo Act and replace it with the Non-Intercourse Act. This law restricted trade with France and Britain only, allowing United States ships to trade with other countries. The Non-Intercourse Act would allow trade to resume with either France or Britain as soon as they eased their restrictions against the United States.

Meanwhile, John Calhoun was busy with his new career. In October 1807, Calhoun was elected to his father's former seat in the state legislature. Not long after that, one of his cousins, Joseph Colhoun, retired from the U.S. House of Representatives. It was thought that his young kinsman, John Caldwell Calhoun, would make a fine successor. Calhoun was certain that he would win by a good margin.

It was more than a good margin; it was an overwhelming margin. Calhoun did have the advantage of his family connections, but it was his stand on the question of war with England that caught people's attention. They wanted a war, and they elected John Calhoun to push for it.

But in spite of all his political success, Calhoun longed for a home life. He was used to living in a house, with a family. Although he had been living on his own for years, he could remember how happy he had been growing up on the farm. He could remember Floride Colhoun, her elegant house and her children. It was time for him to settle down and start his own family.

In the spring of 1809, Calhoun went to visit Floride Colhoun again. It was four years since he had first stayed with her. He had visited since then, but this particular trip was different.

Floride's children were growing up. Little James Edward was 10 years old now, and John Ewing was 17. But Calhoun noticed the biggest change in the younger Floride. When he had first met her she was a little girl of 12. Now, she had grown into a vivacious 16-year-old, the image of her mother. John Calhoun fell in love.

For Calhoun actually to court Floride, he needed permission from her mother. Floride Colhoun was undoubtedly pleased by Calhoun's interest in her daughter. She had enjoyed his company and his correspondence, but a mother had to be careful. She asked Calhoun to wait before he spoke to Floride.

After a few months, Floride Colhoun consented to have Calhoun court her daughter. But it was not until January that he was able to visit the Colhouns again. When he did, he asked Floride to marry him. To his relief, she answered yes. They waited a whole year to be married, but John wrote faithfully to her. "It gives me much satisfaction that time and absence made no impression on my love for you; it glows with no less ardour than at the moment of parting, which must be a happy omen of its permanent nature."

Calhoun purchased a small plantation in the up-country. He and Floride spent the first months of their marriage putting the house in order. Just before he was due to leave for Washington, D.C., Floride gave birth to their first child, a boy. They named the baby

Andrew Pickens Calhoun, after one of the heroes of the Revolutionary War, a famous ancestor of John Calhoun. Calhoun was late leaving for the capital because he stayed a few days longer to make sure that Floride and little Andrew were safe and sound.

In the fall of 1811, Washington, D.C., saw a startling change in the Congress. Nearly half of the congressmen were new to their jobs. Almost all of them were elected because they were pro-war.

The first order of business for the House of Representatives was to elect the Speaker of the House. They chose a brash new representative from Kentucky named Henry Clay.

Henry Clay was just 35 at the time. He had been born in Virginia, but he moved to Kentucky when he was 20 years old. Lexington, the town he moved to, was exactly the same age as Clay. It was a place filled with excitement, constantly changing and growing. The riches of the West gave the people money to burn in Lexington. Gambling and racing were favorite pastimes. Henry Clay loved it. Before he was 30, he was one of the leading lawyers in the state.

Henry Clay was elected to the state legislature when he was 26. A few years later, in 1806, he was appointed to fill a seat in the U.S. Senate. He was actually four months too young to hold the post legally, but nobody bothered to check his age. They were too impressed by his personality, which was aggressive, outgoing, and charismatic. In 1811, Clay left his seat in the Senate and was elected to the House of Representatives.

As soon as Clay was elected, the senior members of Congress could feel the change. The second order of business was for the Speaker to assign members to various House committees. Each committee would review the bills proposed and report on them to the House. Clay, feeling certain that he would be chosen as Speaker, had already made his list of appointments. But the senior members were alarmed. One rose to suggest that the Speaker wait at least until the next day to announce his appointments.

Henry Clay saw no reason to wait. He had already made up his mind. The older members watched helplessly as Clay brushed seniority aside. He gave the important appointments to the young freshmen. The new members of Congress had taken control.

Congressman Henry Clay of Kentucky, speaker of the House and leader of the War Hawks.

Two days after Henry Clay was elected, John Calhoun arrived in Washington. The two men found that they worked well together. Calhoun was quietly serious, while Clay was expansive and outgoing. Calhoun was logical and careful; Clay was fiery and quick-witted. Calhoun, despite his high-country upbringing, appeared to Washington as the embodiment of Southern gentility, while Clay represented the vitality and vigor of the new West. Together, they would lead the war movement.

Since Washington was a relatively new town, private homes were rare. Most Congressmen left their families in their home states, while they stayed in boardinghouses. Henry Clay invited Calhoun to rent rooms at the place where he was staying.

By chance or on purpose, the leading congressmen of the war movement were all staying in that house. It soon became known as the "War Mess" ("Mess" is a military term for a place were soldiers eat together.) It was at the War Mess that John Calhoun first met William Lowndes, a fellow South Carolinian. Lowndes was a tall, frail man, serious in his manner and modest in his conversation. Calhoun and Lowndes became instant friends. The very next day, Lowndes wrote of Calhoun, "I like him better than any member of our mess and I give his politics the same preference."

Henry Clay placed John Calhoun on the foreign relations committee. It was this committee that would review bills relating to the impending war.

The war movement did have opposition, especially from a man named John Randolph of Virginia. Congressman John Randolph was one of the more interesting people in Washington. He could trace his heritage back to Pocahontas and John Rolfe. His figure was tall and spindly, his face both wizened and childish. He was eccentric and unsteadily brilliant, and he was dead set against another war with Britain.

Even though he was a Republican, Randolph started an anti-war movement, backed up by the Federalists. He attacked the "War Hawks," as the supporters of the war movement came to be known, for pushing the country into a war it was not prepared for. He sneered at Calhoun's concern over impressment, coming as it did from a inland farmer "who never saw a ship." He accused both Clay and Calhoun of using the war issue as a stepping-stone to the presidency. He even claimed that a comet that was sighted then meant the United States should avoid conflict with Britain.

This was too much for Calhoun to take quietly. "Are we to renounce our reason? Must we turn from the path of justice...because a comet has made its appearance...?" he asked.

In December, the foreign relations committee released its report to the House. Randolph rose to speak against it. He demanded to know if the report actually meant war. How could the United States declare war when it was so unprepared for it? Who would support it? Not the merchants of New England. They were starving for lack of trade. Nor could the Southern planters afford the taxes necessary for the conflict.

Why help the French? The vision of the French Revolution still haunted Americans. Randolph added to their fears. What if France's dangerous ideas of liberty spread to the slaves? What would happen to the helpless wives and children of the masters while they were away fighting? "The night-bell never tolls fire in Richmond that the mother does not hug the infant more closely to her bosom," he ranted.

It strained John Calhoun to the breaking point to listen to this. It was even worse to see Randolph's words filling the columns of the newspapers day after day. Calhoun and the other War Hawks had been elected to start a war. But for the war to succeed, the will of the American people would have to be behind it. Calhoun was convinced that Randolph might harm the morale of the country with his wild outbursts. But he waited quietly until Randolph had finished, then rose to reply.

Calhoun agreed that the report did indeed advocate war. But he argued that the war was necessary. The United States could not just let the British kidnap its citizens. "If our country is unprepared," he said, "let us remedy the evil as soon as possible." He argued that when independence and patriotism were involved the citizens of the United States would not hesitate to pay the necessary taxes. "I cannot dare," he thundered, "to measure in shillings and pence the misery, the stripes and the slavery of our impressed seamen; nor even to value our shipping, commercial and agricultural losses, under the Orders in Council and the British system of blockade."

"If he really wishes to promote the cause of humanity," Calhoun suggested, referring to Randolph, "let his eloquence be addressed to Lord Wellesley or Mr. Percival, and not the American Congress. . . . Let melting pity, a regard to interest of humanity, stay the hand of injustice, and my life on it, the gentlemen will not find it difficult to call off this country from the bloody scenes of war."

As Calhoun finished his address, the members of the House swarmed around him, caught up by his speech. This new member of the House, barely a month in Congress, daring to go up against John Randolph! Not just daring, but actually besting him in debate. It was a thrilling moment.

Calhoun himself was also elated. It had been his first big speech to the House. He had never thought of himself as a public speaker. He was too rational and precise—too dry. His talents were in logic and organization, not in the dramatic flair that captivates an audience. But today, his arguments had been backed up by passion, and he had risen above his usual style. An editor, observing the moment, predicted that Calhoun would become "one of the master spirits, who stamp their names upon the age in which they live."

THE WAR OF 1812

"We in New England are not patriots—we will
do what is required—no more."

DANIEL WEBSTER

On June 1, 1812, the foreign relations committee of the House of Representatives received a message from the president supporting the declaration of war. Two days later, John Calhoun, now the head of the committee, submitted a war report to the House. The report concluded that war was the only way to resolve the problems between the United States and Britain. The next day, the House voted to declare war.

On June 18, 1812, President Madison signed Congress's bill into law. He had just declared war against the nation with the most powerful navy in the world, the nation that was the United States' most important trading partner. Although no one knew it, the justification for the war no longer existed. On June 17, even before its members could have heard about the House vote, the British Parliament had repealed the Orders in Council.

The war stirred up the patriotism of many people in the United States. They saw the war, as John Calhoun did, as a "Second American Revolution." They thought the war would soon be settled in the United States' favor. In Boston, a verse was published to cheer the United States forces on:

Since war is the word, let us strain every nerve
To save our America, her glory increase;
So, shoulder your firelock, your country preserve,
For the hotter the war, boys, the quicker the peace.

At first, the war was mainly fought in the North, in Canada. American General Henry Hull led 2,000 troops across the Detroit River into Canada, but they did not get far. The British commander, General Sir Isaac Brook, not only stopped the invasion, but drove the United States forces back across the river and into Detroit, which he then surrounded. General Hull had to surrender the city and the army to the British. The British army, allied with Native Americans and Canadians, also took the settlements of Michilmackinac and Fort Dearborn (now Chicago).

In Kentucky, Major Samuel Hopkins was ordered to lead 4,000 troops to avenge the defeat at Fort Dearborn. After five days, the troops threatened mutiny. Hopkins's officers advised him to retreat. Scornfully, Hopkins called out his troops. He made an impassioned speech to his men, asking for 500 volunteers to lead the charge. Not one man stepped forward.

On the other hand, the United States Navy, which had been neglected compared with the army, had won some surprising victories. In July, a British attack on a U.S. naval base was stopped by the gunfire of one American ship, the *Oneida*. In August, General Henry Hull's nephew, Captain Isaac Hull, in command of the *Constitution*, fought with the British frigate *Guerriere* off the coast of Nova Scotia, destroying her and taking the crew prisoner.

But the conflict was hampered by the New England states. The Federalists were still against the war, even after it began. To begin with, they believed the campaigns in Canada were inspired not so much by patriotism as by simple greed. They accused the War Hawks of waging the war as an excuse to annex Canada to the United States. They refused to send troops to fight.

When John Calhoun himself returned to Congress in the fall of 1812, he noticed the absence of one important member. His greatest opponent, John Randolph, had been defeated in the fall election.

John Calhoun had nearly not returned. During the census of 1810, Calhoun's district, Abbeville, had been combined with another congressional district. That meant General William Butler and John Calhoun were sharing the same seat in the House. As the younger member, Calhoun should have been the one to step aside. But General Butler stepped down. He realized that Calhoun's talent and energy were needed in the House. General Butler retired from Congress to fight in the war.

Immediately after President Madison signed the declaration of war, Calhoun had moved to repeal the embargo the president had imposed to try to prevent the war. By opposing the embargo, Calhoun was going against his own party. The Republicans thought the embargo was a good economic weapon against England. But Calhoun felt the embargo violated the principles of free trade.

Calhoun was also reaching out to the Federalists. Their criticism of the war was getting more and more vocal. Calhoun knew from his experiences at Yale and Litchfield how eager the Federalists were to secede from the Union. More than anything, he was afraid that opposition to the war could lead to disunion. "This single word comprehended almost the sum of our political dangers," he later said, "and against it we ought to be perpetually guarded."

The Federalist opposition to the war was not limited to the Congress. In 1812, the United States Army occupied Queenston Heights on the Canadian side of Niagara, but it needed reinforcements to hold its position. The commander asked the New York militia for help. New York was a Federalist state and opposed the war. The troops arrived, but they refused to fight. From the New York side of Niagara, they watched as their fellow countrymen were overwhelmed and forced to surrender.

By repealing the embargo, Calhoun hoped to win the Federalists over. He believed that once the Northern merchants were not distracted by economic concerns, they would support the war for the justice of its cause. But in spite of all his efforts, the House voted down Calhoun's proposal.

Calhoun also supported shippers concerning the Non-Importation Act. When England had repealed the Orders in Council the preceding spring, U.S. ships in that country had rushed back with full holds of English goods. When they arrived in the American ports, they found the nation at war. The American navy seized their cargoes; the United States levied heavy fines against them. Calhoun got the government to release the impounded ships and return the fines to the shippers.

This move had been opposed by Speaker Clay as well as by the administration. The amount of the fines added up to $15 million, money desperately needed by the country to finance the war. Although Congress had passed a bill the year before that increased the number of troops in the army, actually finding the soldiers to fill the ranks had proved impossible. Now, a year later, the ranks of the army were still only half full. The pay for a soldier had already been raised to $8 a month, but Congress authorized even more. Each soldier who enlisted would receive a cash bounty of $24 and 160 acres of land upon discharge. In addition, he would be exempt from imprisonment for debt.

The Federalists opposed these measures. They accused the administration of raising the army in order to occupy the New England states and squelch the opposition to the war. They were strengthened by the arrival of Daniel Webster of New Hampshire in the spring of 1813. With his piercing black eyes and wild hair, his deep, sonorous voice and dramatic style, he appeared to Washington not so much a man as a force of nature.

Henry Clay appointed Webster to the foreign relations committee. Webster used the committee to promote an attack on President Madison. In 1810, Napoleon Bonaparte had supposedly repealed his Berlin and Milan Decrees, which meant that American ships could legally sail into French ports. However, Napoleon had apparently given this information to Madison secretly. Webster accused President Madison of deliberately keeping the repeal of the decrees from the British. He argued that if the British had known about the repeal of the decrees, they would have revoked the Orders in Council and averted the war.

Although Calhoun did not support Webster's claim, the committee agreed to pass his resolution calling for an investigation. After several days of intense debate, the resolution passed the House, so

Daniel Webster often opposed John Calhoun in debate on the Senate floor.

that other, more pressing, business could be attended to. But many in the House, including Speaker Clay, were disgusted by the accusation. Clay ordered Webster to present the resolution to Madison himself.

When Webster arrived at the President's Mansion (as the White House was known then), he found Madison sick with malaria. But the president managed to send a letter to the Congress within six weeks. The letter explained the whole affair. In actuality, Napoleon's repeal of the decree had been a lie. The French dictator had only pretended to repeal the decrees so that trade with the United States could continue.

But Britain had never believed that Napoleon was serious in the first place. They had not repealed the Orders in Council or stopped their harassment of U.S. ships. The grievances against Britain remained as strong as ever.

After the bitterness and division caused by Webster's action, John Calhoun thought things could not get any worse, but by the time he returned for the fall session, a disaster has occurred. That summer, the U.S.S. *Chesapeake* had been attacked and captured by the British. Captain James Lawrence, a celebrated American naval hero, had been in command and was mortally wounded during the battle. The *Chesapeake*, the ship that had become the rallying cry of the War Hawks after its surprising, against-the-odds triumph, was now a British prize.

But in January 1814, Madison received good news. The British were interested in resolving the war peacefully. They asked the United States to negotiate directly. President Madison accepted the offer. He appointed a four-man peace commission that included John Quincy Adams and Henry Clay.

John Quincy Adams was the son of John Adams, the second president of the United States. As a child, he had traveled with his father to France. At 14, he was already working as the private secretary to the first American diplomat in Russia. John Quincy Adams returned to the United States as a young man. He graduated from Harvard, studied law, and started his own practice. But he was born to public service, and by the time he was 25, he was the American minister to the Netherlands. He also served as minister to England, Portugal, and Prussia. During Thomas Jefferson's administration, he represented Massachusetts in the Senate. His experience and knowledge of European affairs made him a perfect choice for the peace commission.

Henry Clay was a wild card. He had no experience in negotiating a peace treaty. He had never even left North America. But Henry Clay represented the West, which was growing into an important region of the country and deserved representation at the peace talks. Also, Clay had his own special talents and experience

H.M.S. *Shannon* (center) leads the captive frigate U.S.S. *Chesapeake* (far left) into Halifax Harbor, June 6, 1813.

to contribute. He had grown up in the rough–and–tumble world of the West, getting his education at the gaming tables and racetracks. Though a backwoods gambler might not make a very good role model, as a negotiator he had tremendous advantages. During the talks, he told Adams that they reminded him of the game called "brag." Adams recounted: "He asked me if I knew how to play brag. I had forgotten how. He said the art of it was to beat your adversary by holding your hand with a solemn and confident phiz [face] and outbragging him."

That was precisely what they did. They met the British ministers in the little town of Ghent, Belgium. The delegation from the United States did not have much to bargain with. The army had met defeat after defeat. The embargo had been a failure, hitting the merchants of the United States far harder than the British. The opposition to the war from the Federalists under-mined any efforts at national unity. As the peace commission began its work in August 1814, the members of the United States delegation knew they would have to outbrag the British.

HARTFORD, NEW ORLEANS, AND GHENT

"No foreign foe had broken my heart. To see the
capital wrecked by the British does not hurt so
deeply as to know sedition in New England."

JAMES MADISON

Late in August 1814, the British entered Washington, D.C.,
spreading terror and confusion and putting the citizens to
flight. Dolley Madison, wife of the president, had just set
the table for supper when she received a penciled note warning her
to be ready to flee. Forgetting the meal, she hurriedly supervised
the servants in gathering the china, silver, and other valuables. She
waited as two workmen cut the portrait of George Washington out
of its frame, then caught the canvas and carried it with her out of
the city.

The British marched into Washington on the heels of their
commander, Admiral Sir George Cockburn. He rode on a white
mare, whose foal followed along, trying to nurse. The British fired
upon the Capitol building, and once inside, Admiral Cockburn
climbed to the speaker's rostrum and called his troops to order. He
put the question, "Shall this harbor of Yankee democracy be
burned?" and at their cheers, he declared the motion carried
unanimously.

The British indulged themselves in a riot of destruction. They
pulled the books from the Library of Congress, the paintings from

the walls, the carpets from the floor, and combined them in a huge
bonfire. They set fire to the Capitol itself, while Admiral Cockburn and his troops sat down and ate the dinner left by Dolley
Madison on the table in the White House.

When John Calhoun arrived in Washington that fall, the city was
just beginning to recover from its sacking. Congress was meeting
in a building that had been a post office, a patent office, a theater, a
lodging house, and a tavern. Now it was the Capitol. The House of
Representatives met in a tiny room with one small fireplace. By the
time John Calhoun arrived, a month late for the session, all the seats
had been taken. He had his choice of the window ledge or the
fireplace.

As he took his seat, he found the congressmen in heated debate.
Since the Congressional library had been burned, Thomas Jefferson
had made an offer. He would sell Congress his entire library, which
consisted of more than 6,000 volumes. Some members objected
that the collection contained the works of Voltaire, a French
philosopher. Besides supporting radical political ideas, Voltaire's

works were satiric and many viewed them as obscene. There were those in Congress who wondered if it was proper for the government to have such books in its collection.

As Calhoun looked over the ruins of the nation's capital, it must have seemed absurd that Congress was wasting time debating about Voltaire. There were so many other pressing worries. The army had still raised only a third as many soldiers as it needed. The government was more than a million dollars in debt.

The best chance to raise money seemed to be to authorize a national bank. The first national bank of the United States had been organized by Alexander Hamilton. Its charter had run out in 1811, and because the state banks had opposed it, the charter was not renewed.

Now it was felt that the time had come to re-authorize a national bank. Secretary of the treasury George M. Dallas presented a plan to the Congress calling for a national bank with capital of $50 million. Calhoun found Dallas's plan unsound, but he had one of his own to offer. By the time they finally decided on a plan they could both live with, Daniel Webster had arrived. He rallied the Federalists to defeat the plan. Calhoun was in despair. Impulsively, he rose from his seat and held his hands out to Webster for help. Would he work with Calhoun on a plan for a national bank that both parties could agree to? Webster said yes, but it would be two years before the plan was finally approved.

Webster's help was desperately needed to reconcile the Federalists. The opposition to the war was escalating into talk of secession. When the parties were first formed, during George Washington's presidency, the main issue between Federalists and Republicans had been the central government. In general, the Federalists favored a strong central government. The Republicans believed in the power of the people and felt that a strong central government would infringe upon the natural liberties of the people.

But during Jefferson's presidency, things shifted around. Although the Federalists believed in a strong central government, they drew the line at a strong central government run by Republicans. And as the Republicans became more and more powerful, they stopped having such a deep dislike for government itself.

When Jefferson bought the Louisiana Territory from France in 1803, the New England Federalists became alarmed. They could foresee the country adding state after state, each filled with the evils of Republicanism. Some Federalist leaders met secretly to plan the secession of New England from the rest of the country. They argued that the addition of territory to the United States was not provided for in the Constitution. Buying the territory canceled the New England states' obligation to the country.

Alexander Hamilton was not one of these leaders. Even though he disliked Jefferson and despised Republicanism, he would not let party differences destroy the country. As the founder of the Federalist party, he had a lot of influence. He used that power to stop the plan. Since that time, the Federalists had often talked about breaking from the Union, but it had been mostly talk.

Now, with the war, the Federalists were thinking seriously of secession. They met in December 1814 in Hartford, Connecticut. The convention, known as the Hartford Convention, drew up a report concluding that peace between the United States and Britain was not possible. The five states of Connecticut, New York, Vermont, New Hampshire, and Massachusetts should band together and protect themselves. Since these states refused to contribute any militia to the war effort, their intention could only have been to protect themselves from the federal government itself.

In the meantime, the war continued on the frontier. A new commander, General Andrew Jackson, was beginning to win a few victories. Andrew Jackson had been a child when the Revolutionary War was fought, but he had served as an orderly in the Continental Army. He and his brother were captured by the British army. When 13-year-old Andrew refused to clean an officer's boots, the officer drew his sword on the boy. Putting up a hand to defend himself, Andrew caught the blade, which sliced his hand to the bone. Later, he and his brother were ransomed by their mother, but they all caught smallpox from the British camp. Andrew's mother and brother died, leaving him an orphan at 14.

Jackson then served in the militia in Tennessee. He led 2,500 troops, including Choctaw and Lower Creek Native Americans, to victory against an uprising of the Upper Creek tribes. His success led to a treaty with the Creeks that opened up two-thirds of what later became the state of Alabama.

In 1814, the British landed at Pensacola, which actually belonged to Spain. They joined forces with Creeks and runaway slaves. Jackson invaded the Floridas on his own authority and captured Pensacola.

Jackson guessed that the British would attack Mobile next. He ordered the ships in the harbor at New Orleans to sail to Mobile. But the British had other plans. They met the ships on their way to Mobile and sank them. Jackson then realized that the British were planning to take New Orleans.

There was not much time. General Jackson ordered his troops to start digging and building barricades. They worked all Christmas Day in the freezing cold. But they finished the job. By New Year's Day, three different lines blocked the approach to New Orleans.

In the meantime, the peace commission was dragging on in Ghent. There was not much for the Americans to bargain with, but Britain was tired of war. The two countries agreed to peace based on their relations before the war started. That meant that the central issue of the war, impressment of American sailors, was not decided in the United States' favor. Britain still asserted her right to seize deserters. In the end, the peace settlement rested on two issues: fishing rights, and navigation along the Mississippi River.

Before the war, New England fishermen were allowed to sail the northern Canadian waters freely. But Britain now took away that right, since the United States had invaded Canada.

The British right to navigate the Mississippi seemed unimportant. The British did not claim any land below the 49th parallel. They had no need to travel on the Mississippi. But Clay knew how the British traders exerted pressure along the frontier. They provided Native Americans with guns in exchange for animal pelts. If the British were allowed on the Mississippi, they could seriously hinder American expansion in the West.

In the end it was agreed to deny both rights. The New England fishermen could no longer fish the waters of Newfoundland, and the British were not allowed free navigation of the Mississippi. The treaty was sent to Congress for ratification.

As the news of the treaty traveled across the ocean to the United States, British troops were arriving at New Orleans. The British stormed the barricades that Jackson built, but the lines were well placed and well defended. The British fell back and waited for reinforcements. In the meantime, Jackson continued to build up the defenses.

Finally, on January 8, 1815, the British attacked for the last time. In the battle, 2,000 British and colonial troops were killed, wounded, or missing. Among the dead was the commander, General Sir Edward Pakenham. Only 13 soldiers in Jackson's army were killed, and only 58 more were wounded. Jackson's victory at New Orleans was the biggest success for the United States in the whole war.

News of these three events—the Hartford Convention, the Battle of New Orleans, and the Treaty of Ghent—reached Washington almost simultaneously. The effect was one of overwhelming relief. After two years of military failures, bitter party division, and despair, the Battle of New Orleans and the Treaty of Ghent were welcome climaxes. Nobody seemed to mind much that the treaty resolved none of the issues of the war, or that since the battle had happened after the treaty, the battle had been unnecessary. The important thing to everyone was that the two events restored American pride.

The Hartford Convention might have led to a real crisis if the Treaty of Ghent had not been signed. As it was, it merely stood as a reminder of the resistance of the Federalists to the national cause. It nearly ended Daniel Webster's political career, not because he had actually been involved in the convention, but because he had allied himself with the Federalist cause. It was an embarrassment to the Federalist party, one from which it never recovered.

So ended the War of 1812, a war fought for the rights of seamen who neither asked for it nor supported it, a war fought for territory between countries that left the boundaries exactly where they had stood before. This was a war called for by men using the war cries

At the Battle of New Orleans, Andrew Jackson's outnumbered forces defeated the British troops.

of the Revolutionary War, who had only been babes in arms when the revolution was fought, a war that was really fought for something intangible—self-respect. And in that one regard, the United States succeeded. The United States came out of the war with a renewed sense of nationality and pride. With the end of the war, the people of the United States felt that their country was ready to stand up to any other in the world.

6

BUILDING A NATION

"These halcyon days of peace, this calm will yield
to the storms of war, and when that comes I am
for being prepared to breast it."

HENRY CLAY

t last the war was over. With relief, Congress adjourned, and Calhoun returned to his home, ready to enjoy the comforts of his family. While he had been away the year before, Floride had given birth to their second child, a daughter. Following tradition, they named the baby Floride. Now Floride was 14 months old, and already beginning to walk and talk.

But sickness was always just around the corner. In April 1815, Calhoun wrote to his mother-in-law, Floride Calhoun, describing the sudden illness of the child. "We suspect no danger till about midnight and even then except a wildness in her eyes the symptoms were not very distressing. We became much alarmed about day; and sent off a dispatch for Dr. Casey but he was gone to Augusta. Everything was done which we thought could be of service but in vain. Thus early was snatched from us in the bloom of life, our dear child whom providence seemed, but a few hours before so destined to be our comfort and delight.... She is gone, alas! from us forever; and has left behind nothing but our grief and tears."

When John Calhoun left for the capital that fall, Floride was again pregnant. The death of their daughter had shaken Calhoun's confidence in country doctors. He ordered Floride to go to Charleston for the birth of the child. And, to relieve the anxiety he felt at leaving her so soon after their tragedy, he begged her to write by every mail.

As John Calhoun traveled to the capital, he passed through a different nation. Wartime demand for cotton had brought a change to the South Carolina countryside. The small fields filled with vegetables, fruits, and cash crops of rice and tobacco had been replaced. White fields of cotton stretched as far as the eye could see.

Jackson's victories in Alabama had opened up a whole new territory in the West. People rushed to settle the land. In time, Alabama would become a leading state in cotton production.

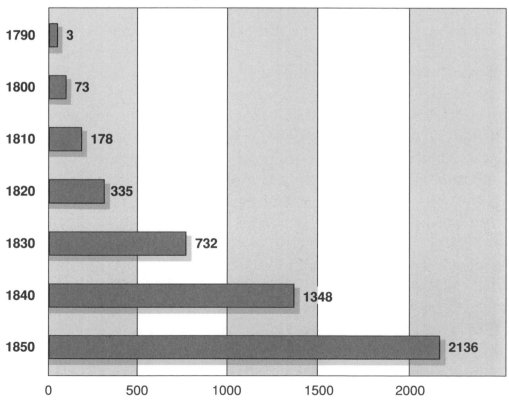

COTTON PRODUCTION IN THE UNITED STATES, 1790–1850
(in the thousands of bales)

Year	Bales
1790	3
1800	73
1810	178
1820	335
1830	732
1840	1348
1850	2136

Another difference that John Calhoun could note was the steamboat. The first successful steamboat, the *Clermont*, had chugged up the Hudson River in 1807. Now, in 1815, Calhoun rode a steamboat for the last 50 miles of his journey to the capital. He arrived a week early for the session. Usually he was late.

The capital city was still showing the scars and burns left by the British, but, after the flush of victory, the peace was like a cool wind, smoothing out disagreements in the Congress. The threat of secession from the Hartford Convention disappeared. People soon settled down to regular business.

But the country had undergone a change that had almost been overlooked in the excitement and disruption of war. The war forced New England, so long a maritime region, to develop new industries. During the war years, the British had blockaded the coast of the United States, and fishing rights in Canada were still denied to fishermen from the United States.

New England had turned its attention inward. Instead of shipping, the region had turned to manufacturing. British goods had been smuggled into the country during the war at very high prices. The high prices allowed New England manufacturers to sell their own goods at a profit and still charge less than the Europeans. It had allowed New England manufacturers and entrepreneurs to develop new factories and new ways of making things. Now the struggling new industries in New England were being threatened by established companies in Europe. The Federalists, who had opposed embargo, non-importation, and tariffs (or taxes on imports) during the war, now needed these measures to protect their products.

Henry Clay was re-elected Speaker of the House. Clay and Calhoun had led the War Hawks during the War of 1812. Now that the war was over, the War Hawks were still in Congress. Their task was no longer war, but the reconstruction of the nation. Clay had already started working on the problem. He came up with a solution that he called "The American System."

Clay believed that the newly created industries in the United States still needed the protection that the wartime tariff provided.

He knew that the growing West needed roads and canals. He wanted a national bank to bind the country together. He felt that government had a definite role to play in encouraging home markets. He wanted the United States to be completely independent of foreign markets. He thought the American System could bring this about by helping the new industries and improving transportation between the different areas of the country.

Clay chose his appointments carefully to promote his American System. He put William Lowndes of South Carolina in charge of the Ways and Means Committee, and he appointed John Calhoun to head a select committee on the national currency. The country was suffering from inflation, or rising prices, and Calhoun's strong leadership was needed to straighten out the situation.

Calhoun saw a national bank as the answer to the problem. Each existing bank had a certain amount of specie—or hard metal currency such as gold and silver coins. The banks could issue paper notes backed by the specie. But the banks had issued so much paper money that the value of the paper notes had gone down. This resulted in inflation.

The national bank would do business only with those banks that also dealt in specie. That way, the other banks, which were issuing too much paper money, would have to change their ways.

Calhoun's bank proposal, which he had worked on with Daniel Webster, was passed by Congress. Calhoun then drew up a bill calling for all government revenues to be paid in legal tender, which was hard coin, Treasury notes, or notes of the bank of the United States. This was all part of the plan to force the banks to use specie. The banks were outraged that their own bank notes could not be used. They used their influence to defeat the bill.

At this point, Calhoun turned, as he had before, to Daniel Webster. Webster was the most powerful Northern representative, just as Calhoun was the leading Southerner. When they united, the combination was hard to beat. The next day, Webster introduced his own bill to the House. It was almost the same bill as Calhoun's, but with the force of the New Englander behind it, the bill passed that very afternoon.

Meanwhile, William Lowndes came up with a revenue program calling for direct taxation. A direct tax calls for citizens to pay money directly to the government according to the assessed value of their property. In the past, the United States government had relied on indirect taxes, by charging duties on goods imported to the country. The reason for the direct tax was to raise money to support a standing army and navy. For the first time, the United States would have an army without a war.

The War of 1812 had proved what John Randolph said all along. The country had not been prepared for war. The American System would remedy that. A standing army would be ready to fight at a moment's notice. Building roads and canals would make it easier for the army to move. Encouraging manufacturers would keep the United States independent in the event of another war.

John Randolph led the forces, chiefly from the West and New England, that opposed Lowndes's proposal. His chief argument was that a direct tax would strengthen the federal government. This would eventually lead to the restriction of individual liberty.

Calhoun spoke in answer to Randolph. He saw a greater danger than that of a strong government—that people would let the government shrink into nothing now that the crisis of war had passed. It was foolhardy to wait for another war before raising the revenue needed to wage it.

Randolph's reply to Calhoun was quite simple. Rather than dispute the merit of Calhoun's intentions, Randolph merely pointed out that direct taxes, the proposed roads and canals, and a subsidized industry would strengthen the national government at the expense of the states. He ended with the warning that the road to power is the road to tyranny. At the time, Calhoun shrugged off Randolph's words. The direct tax was passed.

In the spring of 1817, near the end of the session, Henry Clay proposed a protective tariff. A tariff is a tax on imported goods. This tariff would charge a tax for goods coming in from other countries that competed with similar products made in the United States. This would make the European goods cost more than the

U.S. products, which had no tax charged on them. Clay proposed using the revenue from the tariff to improve roads and canals in the country, making transportation quicker and easier.

John Calhoun was called into the chamber to support the bill. Calhoun argued for the roads and canals as a military necessity. "In the recent war, how much did we suffer for the want of them!" he cried. Roads and canals were also necessary to promote the general welfare. "We are great, and rapidly—I was about say fearfully—growing. This is our pride and danger—our weakness and our strength.... Those who understand the human heart best, know how powerfully distance tends to break the sympathies of our nature.... Let us bind the Republic together with a perfect system of roads and canals. Let us conquer space." With Calhoun's support, the tariff bill passed.

But Calhoun did not stop there. Part of Calhoun's bank bill had required a bonus of $1.5 million to be paid to the government by the chartered bank. Calhoun proposed using this bonus to set up a permanent fund to be used for internal improvements—that is, roads and canals. Calhoun was very persuasive, and Congress passed the measure. But President Madison was not so easily convinced.

Madison had decided to retire. His secretary of state, James Monroe, had been elected to succeed him. On March 1, 1917, Calhoun called upon the president to offer congratulations on his two successful terms. After visiting a while, Calhoun started for the door. The president asked him to come back.

President Madison held Calhoun's internal improvement bill in his hand. He explained that he could not sign it. From his point of view, it was constitutionally unsound. Calhoun had argued that the roads and canals could be justified on the grounds of aiding the common defense and promoting the general welfare. But Madison pointed out that those clauses did not justify any power not contained in Article I, Section 8 of the Constitution—an article that Calhoun believed empowered the government to provide for the nation's defense and welfare. According to Madison, however, the federal government did not have the power to build the roads.

Calhoun was crushed. Madison had been a part of the convention that created the Constitution. It was he who had made sure the Bill of Rights was added. His authority on constitutional matters was not to be questioned. Madison's veto of the bill would be his last official act as president.

Calhoun left the presidential mansion in turmoil. The bank bill, the tariff, and the improvements to roads and canals were all part of the American System. Calhoun was as eager as anyone to support that system. But Calhoun could not forget John Randolph's recent warnings. Now James Madison, the father of the Constitution, had also called the system into question. Were he and the others wrong in pushing the American System so hard?

Calhoun would have been even more disturbed if he had known where the American System was leading. The trade-off of protective tariffs and road building strengthened the alliance between West and North. In time, this coalition would try to force its ideas on the Southern states. The factories—protected by the tariff—would dominate the South, forcing it into colonial status, just as the United States had once been a colony of Britain.

The roads and canals that John Calhoun pleaded for would strengthen the power of the West and North, without doing anything to lessen the differences between North and South. When the country split apart in the Civil War, the internal improvements would help the North crush the South. Without realizing it, Calhoun was helping to bring about the destruction of his beloved South.

THE WAR DEPARTMENT

"If ever there was perfection carried into any
branch of public service it was that which Mr.
Calhoun carried into the War Department."

THOMAS L. MCKENNEY, *Memoirs*

In 1817 James Monroe succeeded James Madison as president. He appointed John Quincy Adams, from New England, to be secretary of state. He offered the position of secretary of war to John Calhoun.

Calhoun hesitated to accept the post. During his six years in the House, he had built a reputation and a following. He had already been re-elected, and he did not need a job. The position of secretary of war was an administrative one, and Calhoun did not have experience in the administration. And the War Department was known to be a disorganized mess. The possibility of failure was overwhelming.

But with the possibility of failure came the opportunity for success. Calhoun was not the sort of man to pass up a challenge. If he could pull the troubled department together, he would prove his ability not just to create laws, but to run the country.

John Calhoun accepted the president's offer and prepared to move his family to Washington. He turned over his plantation to the care of his brother William. Then he and Floride packed up the children and traveled to Washington. While they looked for their

James Monroe, fifth president of the United States, chose John C. Calhoun to be his secretary of war.

own home, the Calhouns stayed with the Lowndes family. On December 8, 1817, John Calhoun was sworn in as secretary of war.

In March 1815, President Madison had asked the Congress to authorize the United States' first standing, peacetime army. The United States had always feared that a standing army would be the first step toward a military dictatorship. No one had opposed the idea more than the Republicans, but things had changed. When he was in the House, Calhoun had proposed that the peacetime army consist of trained officers. In case of war, the army could be expanded with a draft. A draft was a way of forcing citizens to fight in a war, rather than relying on volunteers. It was not a new idea. But the U.S. Army had never used it, even in the darkest moments of the Revolutionary War. In fact, the draft would not be used for many years, not until the Civil War.

When Calhoun took over the War Department, enlistment was below the 10,000-man minimum set by Congress. The army itself was a mass of confusion. Calhoun found more than $45 million in unpaid bills sitting on his desk when he started.

Calhoun proceeded gently, tactfully, and gingerly in his reorganization of the War Department. He presented his changes as suggestions, rather than orders, and coaxed the officers into his way of doing things. The previous secretary of war had insulted General Andrew Jackson by sending orders to his officers, instead of to the general himself. Jackson sent an angry letter to Calhoun, refusing to obey the orders. Calhoun ignored the tone of the letter. He simply sent all his orders directly to Jackson, as should have been done in the first place. Gradually he managed to get the department to run more efficiently and economically.

Calhoun's department was also in charge of Indian affairs. People in the United States were pushing the frontier farther and farther into Native American territory. There were constant battles on the frontier. One of the most troublesome areas was in the Southeast, at the edge of the Floridas.

The Seminole lived in the Floridas, which were a part of the Spanish colonial empire. Runaway slaves from Georgia joined with the Seminole, who sheltered them. Southern slave owners considered this dangerous. Both the Seminole and the black slaves had grievances against the whites—the Seminole because the white people took their lands without compensation, and the slaves because the white people took their freedom without mercy. They often made raids against the settlers.

In March 1818, General Jackson sent a letter to President Monroe. In the letter, he outlined a plan to invade the Floridas and punish the

Seminole. President Monroe never replied to the letter. General Jackson assumed that the president's silence meant that he accepted the plan, so Jackson invaded Florida in May.

When Jackson captured Pensacola, he found two British agitators, Alexander Arbuthnot and Robert Ambrister, among the Seminole and runaway slaves. He shot Ambrister and hanged Arbuthnot.

General Jackson's report threw the Monroe administration into an uproar. John Quincy Adams objected to the barbarity of Jackson's actions in executing the two Englishmen. Both President Monroe and Calhoun supported Jackson's actions as necessary under the circumstances, but Calhoun was upset at Jackson's original invasion of the Floridas. The invasion could be considered an act of war. Whether or not Monroe's failure to answer Jackson's letter signified approval, it was not in the president's authority to declare war on Spain. That power belonged to Congress.

Clearly the situation demanded action from the administration, either to discipline the general or to support his campaign. But James Monroe had already demonstrated his indecisiveness to his cabinet and to Washington. When he convened his cabinet, the controversy deepened.

By now, Adams had changed his position toward the action. The invasion, which he first thought would threaten his negotiations with Spain, was working in his favor. Jackson had acted defensively, not offensively, Adams argued, since the Seminole had been attacking the army. Calhoun pressed the constitutional issue, insisting that the invasion was an act of war. Even Adams had to concede that Jackson could not continue to hold Pensacola without an act of Congress.

As tempers rose in the debate, Calhoun finally demanded that Jackson be censured. To do so would put a mark of disgrace on the general's career and honor. But not to do so might touch off a war—either with Spain over the invasion of its territory, or with Britain over the execution of its citizens.

But both Spain and Britain backed off from a conflict. With Jackson in effective control of the Floridas, Adams was able to force the Spanish minister to agree to give the entire area to the United

States. The British took the position that Ambrister and Arbuthnot were acting without authority. They were not entitled to the protection of the British government. So the danger of war was averted, and the United States gained new territory. The inquiry against General Jackson was dropped. But the incident would have far-reaching consequences for Calhoun.

Another problem that Calhoun faced as secretary of war was constant attack by one of the members of Congress. His name was William Crawford.

Crawford had served as secretary of the treasury under President Madison. He represented a new breed of politician—he saw politics as his profession. He was determined to become president, and his best hope of doing that was to discredit the Monroe administration. Since Crawford was also from the South, he aimed most of his criticism at John Calhoun.

During Calhoun's tenure as secretary of war, Crawford took every opportunity to discredit him. In 1819, a severe economic depression had hit the country. Crawford blamed the depression on the national bank, and he tried to pass the blame on to Calhoun, who had pushed to charter the bank.

Crawford demanded investigation after investigation of the War Department. But Calhoun was not afraid of these attacks. Under his leadership, the department had become so much better organized, and so much more cost-efficient, that he gained rather than lost by the investigations. Still, the annoyance bothered Calhoun, and it was obvious that Crawford made these attacks to discredit Calhoun and the Monroe administration, not to serve any public good.

Crawford's attacks led to a reduction in the U.S. Army troop strength. Calhoun was forced to fire thousands of officers. The worst part was that the number of major generals was reduced from two to one. General Jackson was the second of these. Calhoun either had to fire the general or force him to take a demotion. Jackson chose to leave. The president gave him the governorship of the Florida territory as a consolation.

Still, Calhoun was able to keep the War Department strong. When forced to reduce the army, Calhoun kept as many officers as he could. The army survived with its most intelligent people.

Calhoun's favorite project was the military academy at West Point. Calhoun wanted to attract students from all different parts of the country, particularly from the middle class. He argued that genius was most likely to be found in the middle and lower classes, "not that these classes actually contain a greater portion of talent, but that they have stronger stimulus to its exertion. Rich men, being already at the top of the ladder, have no further motive to climb. It is that class of the community who find it necessary to strive for elevation, that furnishes you with officers...."

Calhoun recommended books for the classes in the academy. He personally interviewed cadets for appointments to the officer corps.

One of the cadets he interviewed was a serious teenager named Robert Edward Lee. Robert E. Lee was one of the success stories of the academy. His family had been leaders in Virginia long before it had even been a state. His father, General "Light-Horse Harry" Lee, was one of the heroes of the Revolutionary War. Robert E. Lee lived up to his family name. He graduated with highest honors in 1829. His career in the United States Army was long and distinguished.

Joseph Eggleston Johnston was another of Calhoun's choices for the officer corps. He was the same age as Robert E. Lee, and he had also been born in Virginia. He graduated from the military academy and eventually became quartermaster general of the U.S. Army.

Still another young man whom Calhoun talked to was Jefferson Davis. Davis was born in Kentucky, but he had grown up in Mississippi. When Calhoun spoke to him, he had already attended Transylvania University in Lexington, Kentucky, for three years. After his graduation, Davis distinguished himself both in the army and in Congress. Under President Franklin Pierce, he held Calhoun's old post, secretary of war.

These three men were bright stars in the military academy that Calhoun fostered. They fulfilled his hopes of what the academy

Jefferson Davis, appointed by John Calhoun to West Point, would become the only president of the Confederacy.

might do to train brilliant future leaders. But in creating these future leaders, the War Department was preparing its own future enemies. For all three of these men would later become leaders of the South in the Civil War. Joseph Johnston led the Confederate armies in Virginia, Tennessee, and North Carolina. Robert E. Lee led the Confederates to some of their most brilliant victories. And Jefferson Davis, the charming young man from Mississippi, became the only president of the Confederacy.

THE MISSOURI COMPROMISE

"This question, like a fire-bell in the night,
awakened and filled me with terror. I considered
it at once as the knell of the Union."
THOMAS JEFFERSON, ON THE MISSOURI QUESTION

J ohn Calhoun's work in the War Department took a toll on his health. For months he worked 14 and 15 hours a day. Finally he made himself sick. On his way back from a visit to his plantation in South Carolina, Calhoun collapsed at a wayside farmhouse. For days he hovered near death.

Floride took over. For most of Calhoun's professional life, Floride had been forgotten. She had stayed, hidden from view, in the isolated up-country. Now, after she had finally joined her husband, he was collapsing from the strain of his job. She took him by the hand and nursed him back from the worst danger.

Calhoun was soon back at his desk, determined to continue his work, but Floride kept a vigilant eye on him. She made sure that he did not skip any meals, and refused to let him work more than six or seven hours a day. She would even interrupt his conferences with Secretary Adams if she though her husband needed a break.

Besides nursing her husband, Floride was an active member of the Washington social scene. She was a gracious hostess, holding parties and dinners at the Calhouns' Washington residence, Oakly. Wives were still a rarity in the nation's capital. Floride often presided at dinner parties where she was the only woman in the company of 10 or 12 men. Floride, who had spent the first 17 years of her life as a pampered Southern belle, and the next seven years practically alone in the up-country, was thrilled at the attention she received.

Washington society did feel fond of John Calhoun and his pretty young wife. Floride was described by a contemporary as "a devoted mother, tender wife, industrious, cheerful, intelligent, with the most perfectly equable temper."

When one of their children, Elizabeth, fell sick, the women of Washington rushed to help the young couple. The president's daughter helped to nurse the child, and the president himself, already concerned about Calhoun's health, called every day. When Elizabeth died, Calhoun's friend William Lowndes took charge of the funeral arrangements, while Calhoun sought to bury his loss under his work.

While Calhoun was busy in the War Department, a crisis was developing in Congress. In 1818, Missouri applied to the United States for admission as a state. This touched off a controversy that pitted the North against the South on the issue of slavery.

The Constitution mentioned slavery only two times. The first was the clause granting representation to the South for slaves: One slave equaled three-fifths of a white man for representation purposes. The second was a clause prohibiting slave trade after 1808. At the time, everyone hoped that the slavery issue would just go away. But slavery was stronger than ever in the South.

The Northern states were committed to fighting the expansion of slavery into the Western territories. Part of their opposition was moral, and part of it was political. When Jefferson wrote in the Declaration of Independence that "all men are created equal," Southerners took that to apply only to white men. But in the North, people took the words at their face value. They did not like the contradiction that their country proclaimed the equality of all men, while enslaving an entire race.

The political part of the opposition came because of the power of the South. The Southern states were given a large number of representatives in the House of Representatives based on the slave population. As the number of slave states increased, the power of the slave states would also increase, overwhelming the nonslave Northern states.

When Missouri asked to join the Union, the Northern states fought Missouri's admission because the state's constitution permitted slavery. The Southern states protested. They said the United States had no right to require a new state to prohibit slavery.

Henry Clay was still the Speaker of the House. He reviewed the question of Missouri. "It is a most unhappy question," Clay lamented, "awakening sectional feelings, and exasperating them to the highest degree. The words *civil war* and *disunion* are uttered almost without emotion." Clay decided that he had to do something to bring people together.

The request of Maine, then a part of Massachusetts, to join as a free state gave Clay an idea. Years earlier, Vermont and Kentucky had joined the Union together—Kentucky as a slave state and Vermont as a free state. When the question of admitting Maine came before the House, Henry Clay announced that, like Kentucky and Vermont, Missouri and Maine would join the Union together or not at all.

The House rejected this idea. But the Senate decided to follow his lead. They linked the two states together. With Missouri and Maine joining the Union at the same time, the political objections to adding another slave state were lessened. The next time the question of Missouri came up in the House, Clay made a major speech, trying to address the moral issues.

Slavery, Clay declared, was a temporary thing. Given time, the institution would die out. But the Union was a permanent concern to everyone. It should not be sacrificed by making attacks on slavery that only drove the sections of the country apart.

Clay's speech was one of his most powerful. But the members of Congress were not about to change their minds. They still could not agree to allow Missouri into the Union. Even though Missouri and Maine were linked together in the Senate, the Senate still could not get a majority to vote to admit the two as states.

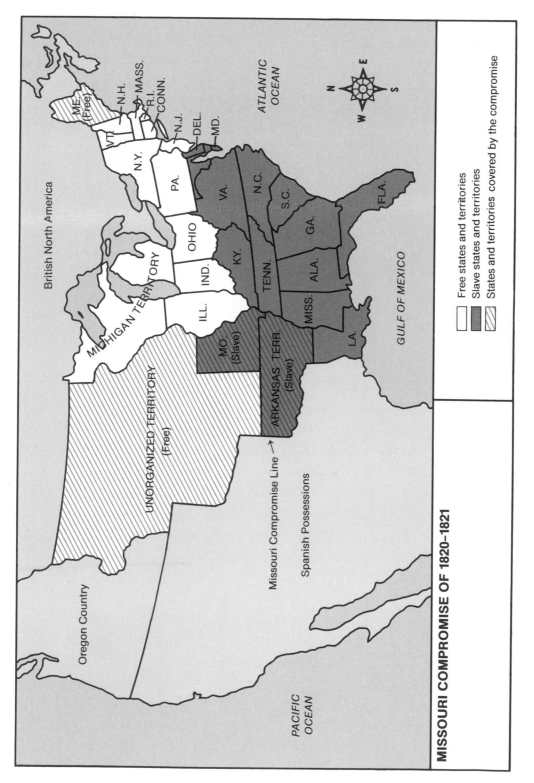

MISSOURI COMPROMISE OF 1820–1821

Free states and territories

Slave states and territories

States and territories covered by the compromise

ATLANTIC OCEAN

British North America

ME. (Free)

N.H.

VT.

MASS.

R.I.

CONN.

N.Y.

N.J.

DEL.

MD.

PA.

VA.

N.C.

S.C.

GA.

FLA.

OHIO

KY.

TENN.

ALA.

IND.

ILL.

MISS.

LA.

MICHIGAN TERRITORY

MO. (Slave)

ARKANSAS TERR. (Slave)

UNORGANIZED TERRITORY (Free)

Missouri Compromise Line

Spanish Possessions

GULF OF MEXICO

Oregon Country

PACIFIC OCEAN

Then another compromise was proposed. In the Senate, an amendment was added to the Missouri–Maine bill. This amendment would admit Missouri as a slave state, but limit the expansion of slavery. The southern boundary of the new state, the 36° 30′ parallel, would mark the northern limit of slavery.

With the addition of this amendment and skillful maneuvering by the bill's supporters, the bill finally passed the Senate. Now it had to go to the House for approval.

The House did approve the compromise. But immediately after the vote was taken, Clay was dismayed to see John Randolph rising from his seat. Clay knew what was coming. John Randolph was opposed to any limits on slavery by the Congress, and he loved nothing better than a good all-out congressional fight. Sure enough, the Virginia representative moved to reconsider the Missouri question.

Luckily, the hour was late. Clay persuaded Randolph to wait until the next morning to make his motion.

The next day, Randolph rose to make his motion again. But Clay was ready. He ruled Randolph out of order. He then proceeded to routine matters, reading petitions that had been sent to Congress. The minutes ticked by. Finally there was no more routine business. Randolph rose again.

It was too late, Clay told Randolph. The bill had already gone to the Senate. Randolph was outraged. He had been tricked. He pleaded with other members of the House to overrule the Speaker. While the House considered this, a page returned carrying the bill. It had been enacted by the Senate. That very day, March 6, 1820, President Monroe signed the bill into law.

Henry Clay hoped that the crisis was over, but his hopes were premature. That summer, Missouri worked out its state constitution. One of the clauses excluded free African Americans from the state. This was an unacceptable violation of the Missouri bill. Free African Americans were citizens in the Northern states, and any right given to any other citizen had to be given to them as well. Congress wanted to strike down the clause. The Southern states saw this as an attack by the federal government on a state's right to self-determination.

Once again, Henry Clay worked out a compromise. Clay managed to get the House to consider a bill accepting Missouri as a state. Missouri could keep the exclusion clause. But it would not be allowed to create laws that restricted the rights of United States citizens, including African Americans.

Three times the bill was defeated. But Clay did not give up. He tried one more time. With a moving speech, he managed to get the House to reconsider the bill one last time. Next he asked for a special committee, composed of 23 members of the House, to review the bill. Then Clay asked for an arrangement entirely new to the Congress. He wanted the members of the committee to be elected by their fellow legislators, rather than appointed. If the members were elected, he could be sure of getting the most popular people in Congress on the committee.

In the committee, Clay won over each member individually until he got the votes he needed. Then he made each member of the majority promise to actively support the bill. With their help, the measure was passed by Congress and Missouri finally entered the Union as a slave state.

But even though the question had been settled in Congress, it was not settled in the hearts of the people. The Southern states resented the whole issue. They felt it was not up to the Northern states to draw a line marking where slavery was and was not allowed. They resented the implication that they could not bring their "property," as they saw the slaves, into free states without the danger of losing them. The issue of the slave trade had been dealt with in the Constitution, but slavery itself had not. The North's objections disturbed the harmony of the states. For the first time, the Northern states had pushed for a measure that directly threatened the Southern way of life.

At his home in Virginia, Thomas Jefferson was appalled at the Missouri decision. He wrote, "A geographical line, coinciding with a marked principle, moral and political, once conceived and held up to the angry passions of men, will never be obliterated; and every new irritation will make it deeper and deeper."

As for John Calhoun, he tried to avoid panicking over the controversy. When his friends asked his opinion, he was careful in his replies. He wrote a friend, "I regret, that any pretext should have been given by the Missouri convention, by which, an objection might be raised to her admission; but I do hope, that all that is virtuous or considerate in the non–slaveholding States, will in every shape discountenance the renewal of so dangerous a question."

Still, Calhoun was alarmed by the Missouri question. He continued, "I can scarcely conceive of a cause of sufficient power to divide this Union, unless a belief in the slave holding States, that it is the intention of the other States gradually to undermine their property in their slaves and that a disunion is the *only means* to avert the evil. Should so dangerous a mode of believing once take root, no one can calculate the consequences...."

Everyone hoped that the question would go away after Missouri was admitted. But the issue of slavery was not so easily disposed of. With the Missouri question, battle lines were draw. As time passed, the different positions would become more and more entrenched. The Missouri Compromise, like the original constitutional compromises, only postponed the conflict over slavery.

ELECTIONS AND POLITICS

"Never in any country, in my opinion, was there in so short a period, so complete an anarchy of political relations. Every prominent public man feels that he had been thrown into a new attitude, and has to re-examine his new position, and reapply principles to the situation into which he was so unexpectedly and suddenly thrown."

JOHN C. CALHOUN

In 1820, the campaign for the presidential election of 1824 began. James Monroe had just been elected to his second term. Jefferson and Madison had been very clear in suggesting their successors, but Monroe refused to do so. For the first time in decades, the election was open. And, although the election was four years away, there were already several strong contenders.

The first of these was John Quincy Adams. As secretary of state, he held the traditional post of presidential successors. But although Adams was respected, he was not well liked. His caustic wit and cold manner did not help him in assuming a leadership role. There were several other popular candidates.

One of these was Henry Clay. The Missouri Compromise had lost him support in the South, but to many he was the personification of the West. His years in the Congress had built up a group of supporters that could not be discounted.

Another candidate was William Crawford. Crawford had first run for president in 1816. Before that, he had served as envoy to France and as secretary of war. Physically, he was large and powerful. Politically, he was a formidable contender.

The last candidate was General Andrew Jackson. He based his candidacy on his popularity and military victories.

Both Adams and Crawford sounded out Calhoun for support. Although Calhoun was a close friend of Adams, he was not sure that Adams would make a good president. On the other hand, Calhoun hated Crawford.

Calhoun's friends and associates suggested that Calhoun offer himself as a candidate. Calhoun consulted his old friend William Lowndes. He was pleased to hear that Lowndes supported the idea. Calhoun gave permission to a group of Congressmen to regard him as a candidate.

It was not long afterward that Lowndes received a surprising message: The South Carolina legislature had unanimously nominated him for president. Lowndes was one of the most respected men in the government, and had even been compared to George Washington for his moderate nature. His supporters believed that if he was made chief executive, he could unite the country again, just as Washington had done. The period of turmoil would be at an end.

After he received the news, it was Lowndes's turn to consult Calhoun. The two talked over the whole situation, weighing the pros and cons. That same day, Lowndes wrote back to the legislature.

In the letter, Lowndes protested that he did not seek the presidency. But he did not decline. "The presidency of the United States is not, in my opinion, an office to be either solicited or declined."

It was traditional for candidates to show a certain reluctance to run for president. Lowndes, however, was sincere. He recommended that the legislature choose Calhoun instead, saying, "I should greatly prefer his election to that of any of his competitors for the office." But South Carolina continued to support Lowndes.

By this time, the business of Congress had turned into a circus. With so many candidates vying for the presidency, the legislature became an exercise in power plays. Crawford and his supporters denounced Jackson, Adams, and Calhoun at every opportunity. Clay's supporters did the same. These attacks were answered by congressmen who favored the others. The seriousness of these rivalries was underscored by a duel fought between one of Calhoun's supporters, George McDuffie, and Colonel William Cumming, a supporter of Crawford.

McDuffie was a protégé of John Calhoun. As a boy, he had worked for Calhoun's brother James. When a seat in Congress became available, McDuffie was elected with Calhoun's backing. Of average height, with blue eyes and black hair, the young man was harsh, abrasive, and unrelenting in debate. But he was devoted to Calhoun. In the duel, McDuffie was wounded—and crippled for the rest of his life.

McDuffie was not the only one to suffer during the campaign. As the election wore on, Lowndes began to fade away. His health, which had never been very good, grew worse. By April 1823, Lowndes was unable to continue in Congress. He requested a leave of absence. On May 1, he resigned his seat. That October, he set out with his family by ship to Europe to recover. He died six days into the voyage.

By 1824, the field was down to Clay, Crawford, Adams, and Jackson. Calhoun realized that he did not have enough support to win the presidency. But he was the clear choice for vice-president.

In the election, Andrew Jackson won the most electoral votes— 99. Adams was next with 84, and Crawford received 41. Henry Clay won only 37, but he was very important to the race. Although Jackson had gotten more votes than any other candidate, he did not have more than half of the votes cast. The decision was sent to the House of Representatives. There, each state would have one vote for president. Clay's influence in the House was strong. Whoever he supported would have a good chance of winning.

Now Clay faced a dilemma. He was not fond of either Jackson or Adams. Jackson won the popular vote in the election, but electing Jackson president could be dangerous. Clay was very suspicious of a president whose claim to the office was based on military victories. Back when Jackson had invaded the Floridas, Henry Clay had warned the House, "Beware who you give a fatal sanction, in this infant period of our republic, scarcely yet two-score years old, to military insubordination. Remember Greece had her Alexander,

Rome her Caesar, England her Cromwell, France her Bonaparte, and that if we would escape the rock on which they split, we must avoid their errors." Clay hardly had to go back all the way to Rome and Greece. Bonaparte was bad enough. After the French Revolution, Napoleon Bonaparte had seized control of the government. He led war after war, trying to conquer all of Europe and even Egypt. He was finally defeated, but not until hundreds of thousands of people throughout Europe had suffered the horrors of war.

In the end, Clay supported Adams, the safest choice and an experienced leader. In doing so, Clay angered those who felt that Jackson should have been elected. To make things worse, Adams appointed Clay secretary of state. To many people it seemed like an out-and-out deal: Adams had given Clay the post in exchange for his support.

Calhoun was among those who felt Clay had made such a trade. Intellectually, he thought it was important for the country to elect a Northern president. John Quincy Adams would be the first Northerner to hold the office since his father, John Adams. But Jackson had won most of the vote. Calhoun wrote of the controversy, "I see in the fact that Mr. Clay has made the Pres't against the voice of his constituents, and that he has been rewarded by the man elevated by him to the first office in his gift, the most dangerous stab, which the liberty of this country has ever received. I will not be on that side. I am with the people, and shall remain so."

Calhoun took his oath of office as vice-president and joined the Adams administration, but his former high regard for the president changed to a deep distrust. Their friendship had already ended when Calhoun refused to support Adams. Now, with the rumors of a "corrupt bargain" between Adams and Clay, Calhoun had also lost respect for the new president.

The government in general was becoming more political. When Calhoun had come to Washington, there were two strong political parties, the Federalists and the Republicans. But after the Hartford Convention, the Federalist party had been doomed. Though the party still existed, its power had dwindled, and it was no longer a

This portrait of John C. Calhoun was painted during his term as vice-president.

serious threat to the reigning Republican party. With a strong opposing party, the Republicans broke up into factions during the 1824 campaign. The only thing most people could agree on was that they did not like John Quincy Adams.

Martin Van Buren, a politician from New York, had supported William Crawford during the campaign. He saw an opportunity in the situation. He would bring together the different groups—Jackson's supporters, Crawford's supporters, and Calhoun's. These groups, all originally part of the Republican party, formed a new political party, the Democratic party.

When the Republic of Panama invited the United States to open diplomatic relations in 1826, Van Buren saw a way to bring Calhoun to his side. He approached Calhoun to oppose the mission. Calhoun agreed to do so. The Senate, not the president, had the power to appoint ambassadors, he argued. Then the foreign relations committee, which Calhoun had loaded with opponents to Adams, submitted a report to Congress. The report condemned the president for usurping the power of Congress by answering Panama's invitation. The report then weighed the consequences of recognizing Panama and decided against sending a mission.

But when the report came up for vote by the Senate itself, Adams and Clay fought back. The issue became the first real political battle of the administration, with Calhoun joining the Jackson–Van Buren side, and Adams and Clay reaching out to the Crawford faction.

Calhoun and Van Buren found a strange ally in the battle—John Randolph. Randolph was now in the Senate, and he was still no friend of Calhoun. He once addressed Calhoun in the Senate as: "Mr. Speaker! I mean Mr. President of the Senate and would-be President of the United States, which God in his mercy avert...." But he was an effective, entertaining, and vocal critic of Adams.

When the resolution from the foreign relations committee reached the Senate floor, Randolph rose to speak. Pacing through the chamber, gesturing wildly, and hurling insults along with his arguments, he spoke against the administration. Other senators tried to stop Randolph by raising points of order, but the president of the Senate, Calhoun, sat motionless and impassive in his chair. Randolph was allowed to continue unchecked, finally going so far as to bring up the accusation of the bargain between Clay and Adams.

Clay replied to Randolph's public speech with a private challenge. On April 8, 1826, the two met by the banks of the Potomac and fought a duel. Neither was hurt. Rumors of duels between Clay and McDuffie, and even between Clay and Calhoun, soon made the rounds.

Calhoun was criticized for his role in Randolph's attack on the administration. It was felt that he should not have allowed Randolph to continue his speech. But Calhoun insisted that he had not had the power to stop the senator. The president of the Senate could not call a member to order, he had decided. Only another member could do that.

By now Calhoun was finding his position unbearable. He was subject to attack on every issue by the president and the secretary of state. His friendship with both men had all but disappeared. The attacks were not just political. Clay's duel with Randolph had been followed by a near-duel with McDuffie, who was already crippled from the duel he had fought during the campaign.

There was only one place Calhoun could turn. In June 1826, he formally wrote to General Andrew Jackson, offering his support in the upcoming election. Jackson wrote back, accepting him as a running mate.

While these political storms were raging, Calhoun was also under stress at home. One of his sons had broken his arm, and another, John, Jr., had gotten a bad cold, which rapidly grew worse. Because of this, John and Floride decided to stay that summer in Washington, rather than return to their home in South Carolina. But as the weeks dragged on, John, Jr., only got worse. The heat and humidity of the Washington air was unhealthful for the child. Finally, the Calhouns decided to return to South Carolina, even at the risk of their son's life. For the first part of their journey, little John's condition worsened still further, but then he rallied. He grew steadily stronger in the cooler, clearer air of the up-country hills.

John and Floride came to a decision. The climate of Washington was poisonous, both politically and physically. The Calhouns decided to keep the children in South Carolina. When Calhoun returned to the capital in the fall, it was without his family.

JOHN CALHOUN AND ANDREW JACKSON

"One man with courage makes a majority."
ANDREW JACKSON

I n the fall of 1827, Calhoun started work in earnest on the Jackson campaign. But his alliance with Andrew Jackson was doomed almost from the very beginning. William Crawford had joined the Democratic party, too, and he and Calhoun hated each other. One or the other would eventually have to go. Martin Van Buren decided that Calhoun would be the one.

In the same year, a letter written to Calhoun by President Monroe was stolen from the War Department's files. The letter concerned the Seminole campaign and seemed to imply that Calhoun had wanted to discredit General Jackson's action. The letter was given to Jackson.

Jackson was insulted and betrayed. He was no politician, unlike Calhoun, Adams, or Clay. He did not understand the difference between a personal attack and a political attack. Calhoun tried to explain in letters that his objection to the Seminole campaign had been based purely on procedure. He had been concerned about the implication that a president could approve an act of war. That power rested with Congress. Calhoun had meant no censure of the general's own actions.

But Jackson was not convinced by Calhoun's explanation. It was an excuse based on politics—and Jackson was a warrior first and a politician second. Although the two men put aside their differences in the interest of unity, their relationship was never the same.

The viciousness of the 1828 campaign made 1824 seem like a garden party. The fight was definitely between two contenders, Adams and Jackson. Jackson's greatest weapon was his personal popularity, and Adams's supporters chose to attack him on just that point. They tried to destroy him personally.

Andrew Jackson's wife, Rachel, had been married once before. She had divorced her first husband to marry the general. Through an error, the divorce had not become final before she and Jackson were married. Although she and Jackson were not aware of the error, this was used against him in the 1828 election. Jackson was accused of having "lived in sin" with his wife.

He was also attacked for having executed six militiamen after they deserted the army. In a handbill decorated with six coffins, the story was told that Jackson had cold-bloodedly murdered six innocent soldiers who had wanted to return home after their terms of enlistment were up. In truth, the soldiers had been fairly tried and found guilty of desertion, which was punishable by death.

Jackson's supporters responded to the attacks in the same way. Adams was accused of having made an improper proposal to an American girl on behalf of the czar while Adams was serving as minister to Russia. And the Jackson supporters in Congress kept up a continual attack on the issue of the "corrupt bargain" between Adams and Clay.

By the time the election was over and Jackson was voted the next president, many people had been harmed by the political battle. One of these was Rachel Jackson. She died of a heart attack less than a month after the election. She had felt responsible for the attacks on her husband. Andrew Jackson, who had loved her deeply, blamed the campaign for her death. "May Almighty God forgive her murderers," he said, "as I know she forgave them. I never can!"

The inauguration of Andrew Jackson began a new era in American politics. In the past, the government had been run

Andrew Jackson, frontiersman and hero of New Orleans, became the seventh president of the United States.

mainly by men of wealth and power, who decided among themselves the outcome of issues. Candidates for public office were chosen by meetings of politicians. The campaigning was done by friends and supporters, rather than by the candidates themselves.

But the election of Adams in 1824 had angered people. They felt that the will of the people had been ignored. When Jackson was elected in 1828, many of the people of the United States felt it was a victory for them, too. They came out in droves to congratulate the new president.

It was a scene that would have confirmed the Federalists' worst nightmares of "mobocracy," or mob rule. Thousands of people thronged the White House for the inauguration. They trampled the flowers, broke the crockery, and left mud on the seats of the White House furniture as they craned to get a view of Jackson. Jackson's address could hardly be heard over the din, and he had to escape from the crowd by climbing out a window.

Jackson appointed one of his oldest and most loyal friends, Major John Eaton, as secretary of war. Eaton had recently married a widow, a pretty young Irish woman by the name of Margaret O'Neill. Everyone who liked her called her Peggy. Everyone who did not called her names that could not be repeated in polite society. Peggy was the daughter of the woman who ran the boardinghouse where Major Eaton lived. He had gotten Peggy's first husband an appointment that called him away from home for long periods of time. People believed the relationship between Peggy and Major Eaton was extremely improper, and many suspected that she had been unfaithful to her husband.

President Jackson supported Peggy Eaton. In his view, the attacks on her were like the ones that had killed his own wife. Most of Washington was ready to condemn her, but the president stubbornly defended Mrs. Eaton's honor, pronouncing her "chaste as a virgin."

Floride Calhoun arrived in Washington for the inauguration. The newly married Peggy Eaton paid a call on Floride. This posed a problem for Floride. Courtesy required her to return the call, but propriety required her not to. To call on a woman accused of adultery would be immoral. It would be condoning sin—and would be nearly as bad as committing the sin itself. On the other hand, there was not positive proof against Peggy Eaton, only highly suspicious appearances. Floride felt out of her element. She did not know enough about the situation to judge, but her action would have great influence on Washington society. She would either condemn an innocent woman or seem to approve of an adulterous act.

Floride put the question to her husband, but John Calhoun also felt himself unfit to judge the situation. He felt that questions of propriety rightly belonged to women, not men. "This is a question upon which women should feel, not think. Their instincts are their safest guides."

President Jackson's cabinet was torn to pieces by the Eaton scandal. Peggy Eaton was snubbed at party after party. Major John

Eaton was furious at the way his wife was treated. The cabinet could not meet because the members could not sit together politely at a table. In a rage, the president wanted to fire the cabinet members whose wives were most opposed to Mrs. Eaton.

Van Buren used the situation to discredit John Calhoun, blaming Floride Calhoun's refusal to call on Mrs. Eaton for the situation. But in fact, the Calhouns had little to do with the issue. They had decided the safest course was for them to return to South Carolina until the matter was resolved. They left town just as the controversy was beginning. While in South Carolina, Floride had given birth to a boy, William. The new child gave her a perfectly good excuse to stay away from Washington—and away from the question of Mrs. Eaton.

Meanwhile, Van Buren struck up a friendship with Peggy Eaton. He knew that would please the president. As John Quincy Adams put it, "Calhoun heads the moral party, Van Buren that of the frail sisterhood." But through his friendship with Peggy, Van Buren won himself an unshakable hold on the general's affections and trust.

After he returned to Washington, Calhoun was handed another letter from the president. It contained a copy of a letter written by Calhoun's old enemy, William Crawford. This letter brought up the old subject of Jackson's invasion of the Floridas. It stated that Calhoun had insisted that Jackson be punished for going beyond his authority. Jackson demanded an explanation.

Calhoun promised to give the president a full answer as soon as possible. But he was alarmed. He had thought the whole affair was dead and buried a year earlier. Clearly someone was trying to destroy his already fragile relationship with the president. Calhoun set out to consult with James Monroe. The former president advised him to give a full explanation. Calhoun wrote a letter to Jackson. He and Monroe had been concerned only about whether it was proper for Jackson to act without direct orders, he wrote. They had defended Jackson's actions when the investigation proved them necessary.

As months went by, Calhoun worked hard to clear up this attack on his character. After his meeting with former President Monroe, he met with other members of the Monroe cabinet. He even met with John Quincy Adams to get the former secretary of state's recollections of the meeting. He finally decided to publish his letters concerning the affair. He asked Adams's permission to publish some of his letters. Adams granted that permission, rather graciously considering his own fights with Calhoun.

Next, Calhoun asked Peggy's husband, John Eaton, to show the manuscript to the president. He wanted to give the president time to review the material and make any changes he felt were necessary. Eaton returned the manuscript after a short while, with a few changes in wording, and Calhoun published it on February 17, 1831.

President Jackson was furious with the publication, and Calhoun realized that he had been tricked. Eaton had never shown the manuscript to the president, or even mentioned it to him. Any hope of reconciliation between the two had effectively been destroyed, and their supporters continued the fight well into the fall. Most people agreed that Calhoun had definitely come off better in the controversy, and Calhoun began to wonder if his chances at the presidency might not be better if he distanced himself from the president, rather than try to make up.

Calhoun felt that he had nothing to lose anymore. His chances of following Jackson as president had been destroyed. Van Buren was now the president's choice as the next president. To top it all off, the president, contrary to his stated position in 1828, was running for a second term.

By now, Calhoun must have been feeling very alone. He and Crawford had always hated each other. Calhoun's friendship with both Henry Clay and John Quincy Adams had been destroyed during Adams's administration. Between Calhoun and Jackson, there was only distrust and dislike. Calhoun's friend William Lowndes had died during the 1824 campaign. His wife and his children had returned to South Carolina. From his high seat in the Senate chamber, the view must have been very lonely indeed.

THE NULLIFICATION CRISIS

"Peace, above all things, is to be desired, but
blood must sometimes be spilled to obtain it on
equable and lasting terms"

ANDREW JACKSON

The Calhouns' flight from the capital during the Eaton scandal brought needed peace to John Calhoun. The political atmosphere of Washington seemed as full of corruption as the air itself was of malaria. In the refreshing climate of the up-country, in the serenity of his country home, John Calhoun's head cleared. He could see the political issues from a wider perspective.

One important issue had been lost in the shuffle of personalities and party. That was the continuing tariff against manufactured goods. The import duties had risen each year, and Northern industries now depended on them. But the tariff had taken a great toll on the economy of the South. The high cost of imported goods made the planter's life more expensive.

The factories of the North did not need as much cotton as the South could provide. The oversupply kept the price of cotton down. Northern bankers would not lend money to farmers who did not plant cotton. This kept the planters from properly diversifying their crops. All these trends combined to trap the South in a system of dependence and poverty from which only the North profited.

At the end of the War of 1812, John Calhoun had welcomed the differences between the regions of the country. Each region was independent, but their needs were complementary. He had hoped the different regions would support each other, allowing each to develop separate identities. But it had not worked out that way. The country was roughly divided into three sections, the North, the South, and the West. A coalition between the West and the North, where the Northern business interests were combined with the Western needs for roads and canals, was serving to oppress the South.

Calhoun saw it all clearly now. The most recent tariff, which came to be known as the Tariff of Abominations, raised the import duty on woolen goods. Between payment of the tariff duties and the devaluation of their cotton, the planters were being squeezed further and further into debt. The growing agitation in the North against slavery seemed to be a plot to further weaken the South. Calhoun decided to fight back. At the request of the South Carolina legislature, Calhoun wrote a statement of Southern grievances.

In the statement, Calhoun did not challenge Congress's power to create a tariff. That was clearly stated in the Constitution. He did, however, deny that Congress had the right to use a tariff to protect one sector of the marketplace—manufacturing—at the cost of another sector, agriculture. Tariffs should be set only to gain revenue, not to provide economic protection.

Calhoun then widened his topic. He protested the tariff as tyranny of the majority over the rights of the minority. But, he warned, the question of minority and majority rights was not limited to the present dispute:

> After we are exhausted, the contest will be between the Capitalists [employers] and Operatives [workers], for into these two classes it ultimately must divide society. The issue of the struggle here must be the same as in Europe. Under operation of the system wages will sink much more rapidly than the prices of the necessaries of life, till the operatives will be reduced to the lowest point, where the portions of the products of their labor left to them, will be barely necessary to preserve existence.

Calhoun felt this breaking down of society into masters and slaves was inevitable because of the nature of man. "Irresponsible power is inconsistent with liberty," Calhoun wrote, "and must corrupt those who exercise it."

But Calhoun had a solution. When the Constitution had first been framed, the states had given up some of their own independence for the sake of union. The powers and responsibilities of the federal government had been spelled out, but those of the states and of the people had not. Calhoun suggested that state conventions, elected by the people to consider a particular issue, could veto acts of Congress. He drew on the precedent of the Kentucky and Virginia resolutions of 1798. Those resolutions had called on the states to assert their power against unconstitutional acts of Congress. But Calhoun went further. He claimed that, since the states had originally given Congress its rights, the states could take those rights away at any time.

In writing this statement in a pamphlet known as *Exposition and Protest*, Calhoun tried to create a way to protect the minority rights of the states, or even a single state, against majority rule. At the moment, the agricultural interests were a minority interest, but that could change in the future. When Congress imposed on the rights of a state, Calhoun wrote, the state could declare that act "null and void" within the state. That meant that the law did not apply within the borders of the state. Calhoun called this idea of a state's veto "nullification."

In 1830, the first debates on the theory of nullification were held in the Senate between Robert Y. Hayne of South Carolina and Daniel Webster of New Hampshire. The theory became widely known and disliked. President Jackson was particularly angry.

In the spring of the same year, John Calhoun attended a dinner in honor of Thomas Jefferson, who had died four years earlier. John Calhoun was seated opposite the president. Martin Van Buren had aroused Jackson's suspicions about Calhoun. He hinted that the vice-president had taken an unnatural interest in Thomas Jefferson, a strong advocate of states' rights. Van Buren led the president into believing that the occasion would be used to justify the nullification theory.

According to custom, the men made toasts after dinner. The first was given to Thomas Jefferson himself, the second to the Declaration of Independence. Those were innocent enough. But as the glasses were raised again and again, the toasts began to support states' rights.

Finally, after 24 toasts, President Jackson rose. His was the first toast not prepared in advance; he had just scribbled the words on the back of the toast list at the table. Raising his glass and staring fixedly at the vice-president, he offered, "Our Union—It must be preserved."

John Calhoun paled. The challenge was obvious. Raising his own glass, Calhoun replied, "The Union—next to our liberty most dear. May we always remember that it can only be preserved by distributing equally the benefits and the burthens of the Union."

As the president and vice-president faced each other off, Martin Van Buren raised a glass, "Mutual forbearance and reciprocal concession: through their agency the Union was established. The patriotic spirit from which they emanated will ever sustain it." Thus Van Buren, who had done his best to create conflict between the two men, offered a toast of reconciliation. But the lines of battle had been drawn, and neither the hero of New Orleans nor the War Hawk of South Carolina was about to step back.

Exposition and Protest had been published anonymously. Calhoun had felt that as vice-president, it would be wrong for him to take credit publicly. But by 1831, after the Eaton scandal and his final breach with Jackson, things had changed. That summer Calhoun worked on a public statement of his position. It came to be known as the "Fort Hill Address." In it, he restated the arguments for nullification that he had used in *Exposition and Protest*.

Within a year, a new tariff bill came up. Jackson signed it into law. South Carolina roused itself to defiance, because South Carolinians believed the tariff would crush their cotton trade. Calhoun's protégé, the hot-headed George McDuffie, immediately called for South Carolina to veto the tariff, even if such an action led to the downfall of federal government. His speech was printed and given out to legislators in South Carolina and the other Southern states.

Calhoun was alarmed at the extreme position that McDuffie was taking. The idea of nullification was to avoid disunion, according to Calhoun. He now felt that he must return to South Carolina. Otherwise, the passions of McDuffie and other extremists might create hostilities between South Carolina and the federal government.

A special session of Congress was called in November 1832, and Calhoun's theories on nullification were put into action. The special session declared the tariffs of 1828 and 1832 null and void after February 1, 1833.

President Jackson's answer to the special session was swift and terrible. "Disunion by armed forces is treason," he growled. He petitioned Congress for the authority to march troops into South Carolina and enforce the tariffs.

Meanwhile, in South Carolina, people were considering how to keep Calhoun, the creator and champion of nullification, in office. Calhoun's term as vice-president would end in March 1833, and it was vital to keep him in Washington. Robert Y. Hayne resigned his seat in the Senate in favor of Calhoun. Calhoun then wrote a terse note to the secretary of state, Edward Livingston.

> Sir,
> Having concluded to accept a seat in the United States Senate, I herewith resign the office of Vice-President of the United States.

It took courage for Calhoun to step into the Senate chamber. The president had actually written to Van Buren that Calhoun "ought to be hung." He may have been making a joke.

But President Jackson was not joking when, in 1833, he asked for troops to invade South Carolina. A resolution known as the Force Bill gave the president power to march federal troops into South Carolina and enforce the tariff.

Calhoun took the floor to oppose the bill. He argued three main points. The first was that the states were parties to a constitutional compact. Since they had agreed to that compact, or contract, they had to abide by it. The second point was that the states delegated certain powers to the federal government. The United States government had the right to act for the states. The third point of Calhoun's speech was that the states were legal judges of which powers they had delegated.

Calhoun's argument, which called the Force Bill a repeal of the Constitution, was powerful. Jackson had to turn to Daniel Webster to defend the administration. Daniel Webster was one of the most powerful speakers in the history of the United States. With his help, the Force Bill was passed.

Calhoun was in a panic. The Senate had condemned nullification. Federal troops stood ready to invade his state. There was nothing he could do—compromise seemed impossible.

But luckily, Henry Clay was now in the Senate, and compromise was Clay's greatest talent. A senator approached Clay, saying, "These Carolinians have been acting very badly, but they are good fellows, and it would be a pity to let old Jackson hang them."

Clay said he would try to work something out. He asked Calhoun to meet with him. Calhoun agreed. They met at night, in secret, and their attitude toward each other was hardly warmer than the winter night. But Calhoun had no choice left but to agree to Clay's terms.

Clay cheerfully set about gathering the forces he needed to work out a tariff South Carolina could live with. In short order, he presented the bill to the Senate. As soon as Clay sat down, Calhoun rose and gave his support to the bill.

Protests immediately arose from New England. Clay was denounced by his own party for abandoning the American System and destroying protectionism. But by now, the Kentucky senator was immune to criticism. "I'd rather be right than be president," he once said.

There was a minor clause in the bill that Calhoun's conscience would not let him vote for. The clause would have created tariffs benefiting some states and harming others. Calhoun felt that it was unconstitutional. He tried to abstain from voting on that particular part of the bill, but the new vice-president, John Middleton Clayton, insisted that he do so. This served no real purpose. It was just a vicious stab at Calhoun by the Jackson administration, and Clay protested. But Clayton was adamant. If Calhoun did not vote on every clause of the bill, Clayton would table it—refuse to let the bill become law. Since Clayton was president of the Senate, he could strongly influence the rules by which laws were passed.

That night Calhoun wrestled with his conscience. He had never before sacrificed his constitutional principles for the sake of politics. On the contrary, nullification was designed to protect the Constitution from disunion. Giving states the right to veto bills was the only way Calhoun could see to keep Southern states from seceding over the question of tariffs. But to obstruct the compromise now, after all Clay's delicate work to build support, would seal South

Carolina's fate. Calhoun had no doubt that Jackson, who had marched his troops into Florida, would march them just as quickly into South Carolina.

In the morning the vote was taken, and with Calhoun's "yes" vote, the measure passed. Within a few days, the entire bill was passed by both the House and the Senate.

Congress adjourned early in the morning of Sunday, March 3, 1833, after sitting all night. Calhoun left immediately for South Carolina. The first part of his work had been done. He had gotten, through Clay's help, a tariff bill that did not promote protectionism. He now had to persuade the nullifiers of South Carolina to accept it.

Calhoun began his trip in a stagecoach, but the vehicle was too top-heavy to maneuver on the ice-covered roads. Calhoun was forced to switch to a mail cart, which was sturdier and faster, but open to the winter air. And, although he was exhausted from the strain of the last months in Congress, Calhoun could not afford to stop or even slow down.

As it was, he arrived at the South Carolina convention a day after it started. He did not speak publicly. Instead, he went from delegate to delegate, persuading each one personally to accept the compromise. The convention did so. It repealed the ordinance calling for nullification, then turned around and declared the new Force Bill null and void. Then the convention was dissolved. The crisis had passed.

But South Carolinians did not forget that the government had threatened their state with martial law. They did not abandon the military preparations they had made under the threat of invasion. The state realized that it might be only a matter of time before the federal government tried again to dominate it. The next time, it would not yield so quickly.

SLAVERY

> "If you put a chain around the neck of a slave, the
> other end fastens itself around your own."
>
> RALPH WALDO EMERSON

In the darkness of a Sunday night in late August 1831, a group of slaves broke into the house of Joseph Travis. They were armed with hatchets and led by a man named Nat Turner. Turner and one other man, Will, sneaked into the bedroom where Travis and his wife slept. Turner struck out at Travis with his axe, but could not see well enough to kill him with the first blow.

"The hatchet glanced from his head," Nat Turner later confessed. "He sprang from the bed and called his wife, it was his last word. Will laid him dead, with a blow of his axe." Mrs. Travis never woke up. She was murdered in her bed as she lay sleeping. Their three children were likewise killed, down to an infant in its cradle. This was the beginning of what came to be know as Nat Turner's Rebellion.

Nat Turner was an astounding character. He was born a slave. Somehow—not even he could remember how—he had learned to read. He could read the Bible and could quote passages from it. When he was a young man, he began to see visions. He spoke of these visions to his fellow slaves, and they began to look upon him as a prophet.

This engraving depicts the capture of Nat Turner, who led a bloody rebellion of escaped slaves.

Eventually, Turner believed that these visions foretold a time, near at hand, when slavery would end. The slaves would rise up and slay their "enemies with their own weapons." When an eclipse of the sun occurred in February 1831, Turner believed that the time for vengeance had arrived. Together with four trusted friends, he started to plan a rebellion.

They originally wanted to begin on July 4–Independence Day. But Turner was ill that day, and the plan was put off. Finally, on the 21st of August, the slaves met in the woods, armed with their axes.

After killing the Travis family, they went on to other homes. Within two days, they had killed 55 men, women, and children. Other slaves and free African Americans joined the band, which eventually numbered between 60 and 80 people.

The revolt was soon put down. A fight at Parker's Field scattered most of the band. Forty-eight people were captured and tried. Nat Turner himself escaped and managed to hide for more than a month.

But he was found at last by a man named Benjamin Phipps. Turner was hiding in a cave he had dug under a fallen tree with his sword. Phipps brought Turner to the town of Jerusalem, where he was tried. Turner confessed to leading the revolt. On November 5, 1831, he received his sentence. The judge, Jeremiah Cobb, ordered "that you be taken hence to the jail from whence you came, thence to the place of execution, and on Friday next, between the hours of 10 A.M. and 2 P.M. be hung by the neck until you are dead! dead! dead! and may the Lord have mercy upon your soul."

Nat Turner's Rebellion terrified the slave owners of the South. For decades, people had thought that slavery would simply disappear, given time. But time had only strengthened the institution.

Some people felt that the answer was to limit slavery to the states where it already existed. They hoped that if slavery were not allowed to grow, it might eventually die out. This movement was called antislavery. Antislavery was not just a Northern movement. In 1827, there were 106 antislavery societies in the slave states.

Some people felt that the answer was to relocate the African Americans to a completely different place, where they could form their own government. In 1816, the American Colonization Society was started. The society acquired land in Africa and created a new country, Liberia. The name Liberia comes from a latin word *liber*, meaning "free." The society began sending African Americans to Liberia in 1822. These African Americans settled there and created their own republic, but many others chose to stay in the United States.

The most radical of the people who opposed slavery were the abolitionists. Abolitionists believed that slavery should be ended completely. One of the most prominent abolitionists, William Lloyd Garrison, published a newspaper called the *Liberator*. It depicted in clear words and pictures the horror of slavery.

Nat Turner's Rebellion changed many people's minds about trying to end slavery. The people who owned slaves became fearful

William Lloyd Garrison created his newspaper *The Liberator* to arouse abolitionist sentiment.

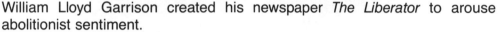

that they might have their own throats slit in the night. They started thinking up ways to keep the African Americans under control.

Even John Calhoun began to notice unrest among his own slaves. His childhood companion, Sawney, who was now known as Old Sawney, still lived on Calhoun's plantation. He had a number of children. One of them, Young Sawney, angered Floride. She threatened to beat him, so he ran away. He was found a few days later in Georgia. Calhoun ordered Young Sawney whipped before he was sent home.

Another of Old Sawney's children, Issey, set fire to Fort Hill, Calhoun's plantation. The penalty for that crime was death by hanging. Issey confessed to the crime, but Floride did not turn the slave over to the authorities. She did, however, insist on selling Issey. John Calhoun refused, but only because Issey was a playmate of his daughter, Cornelia.

Floride blamed the actions of Young Sawney and Issey on their father. She said of Old Sawney, "I think him a dangerous old negro, but cannot convince his Master of it."

After Nat Turner's Rebellion, laws were enacted that stiffened the penalties for slaves who disobeyed their masters. Free African Americans were forced to leave their homes in the Southern states, or else undergo a public flogging. Both free and slave African Americans were forbidden to preach. In the months after the rebellion, dozens of African Americans were shot and killed by panicky white Southerners.

These measures made people take notice. Though slavery had never been right, the rest of the country had tended to overlook the South's "peculiar institution." Even if it was wrong to enslave a human being, at least the slaves were taken care of, fed, and clothed. It was easy for people to persuade themselves that the slaves did not really mind slavery.

But as the masters in the South began to beat and kill innocent African Americans, other Americans became enraged. They saw the denial of human rights to African Americans as an attack on everybody's liberties. In 1835, William Jay, an abolitionist, wrote, "we commenced the present struggle to obtain the freedom of the slave; we were compelled to continue it to preserve our own."

More than a decade earlier, in 1820, the question regarding slavery had been whether it should be limited. The Missouri Compromise had set the northern boundary of slavery at the 36° 30' latitude. At a cabinet meeting called by President Monroe, John Quincy Adams had argued that slavery should not be allowed in a state formed from a free territory.

John Calhoun was also at the meeting. Afterwards, he and Adams walked home together. Adams reported their conversation in his diary. Calhoun, he wrote, "said that the principles which I had avowed were just and noble; but that in the Southern country, whenever they were mentioned, they were always understood as applying only to white men."

Calhoun went on to explain. In the South, all the domestic work—cooking, cleaning, waiting on others—was done by African Americans. "Such was the prejudice," Adams wrote, "that if he, who was the most popular man in his district, were to keep a white servant in his house, his character and reputation would be irretrievably ruined."

Domestic work was seen as degrading, unfit for a free man or woman to do. But other kinds of labor were not viewed that way. Calhoun himself had plowed his own fields. His father had done the same. Other kinds of jobs that required a person to work with his or her hands—even manufacturing and mechanical work—were not considered degrading, only domestic labor was. No white person would stoop to such work.

This, Calhoun explained, kept the white people on an equal footing. Since no white man could serve another white man, he could never call anyone his master. This was the Southern idea of equality—never calling anyone master.

Adams answered shortly that he could not view things the same way. In the North, no labor was viewed as degrading. Society was not considered to be split into servants and masters, but rather workers and employers. Even in 1820, Adams found Calhoun's logic on the subject perverse.

The abolitionist movement really began to grow in the 1830s when the Underground Railroad was started. The Underground Railroad was not a real railroad. It was a name for an organization that helped slaves escape to freedom. There were houses that sheltered slaves on their way to the North. Brave people, some of whom were ex-slaves themselves, guided the slaves.

In the 1830s, abolitionists began flooding Congress with petitions, asking for laws to end slavery. The leading advocate for slavery in Congress was John Calhoun. He said:

I hold that the present state of civilization, where two races...are brought together, the relation now existing in the slave-holding States between the two, is, instead of an evil, a good—a positive good....

There has never yet existed a wealthy and civilized society in which one portion of the community did not, in point of fact, live on the labor of the other....I fearlessly assert that existing relations between the two races in the South, against which these blind fanatics are waging war, forms the most solid and durable foundation on which to rear free and stable political institutions.

Calhoun fought for a "gag rule," a legal measure that would stop the petitions from disrupting congressional business. He also fought to prevent abolitionist literature from being sent through the mail to Southern addresses. Congress voted down the bill to stop the mail, but did approve a gag rule that immediately tabled any petition concerning slavery.

But the abolitionist movement could not be stopped. It found a champion in John Quincy Adams. He went to the heart of the problem when he wrote,

> It is among the evils of slavery that it taints the very sources of moral principle. It perverts human reason, and reduces man endowed with logical powers to maintain that slavery is sanctioned by the Christian religion, that slaves are happy and contented in their condition, that between master and slave there are ties of mutual attachment and affection, that the virtues of the master are refined and exalted by the degradation of the slave; while at the same time they vent execrations upon the slave-trade, curse Britain for having given them slaves, burn at the stake Negroes convicted of crimes for the terror of the example, and writhe in agonies of fear at the very mention of human rights as applicable to men of color.

Adams wanted Congress to hear the petitions. But more than that, he believed that Calhoun's gag rule violated the principle of free speech. He fought the rule, finally overturning it in 1844.

Back in 1820, when John Calhoun and John Quincy Adams were still friends, slavery had been the topic of discussions between them. Even though John Calhoun was a slave owner, they had been able to discuss slavery in a friendly way, as a remote and abstract problem. But time and events had destroyed their friendship. And the problem of slavery was becoming less and less remote. By the 1830s, the defense of slavery had become a passion for Calhoun. But slavery, which had been only distasteful to Adams in 1820, was now impossible for him to accept.

TEXAS AND OREGON

"The annexation of Texas to the Union, and the settlement of the Oregon question on a satisfactory basis, are the great ends to be accomplished."

JOHN TYLER

A fter John Calhoun's disagreement with President Andrew Jackson, he had no choice but to leave the Democratic party. He joined forces with Henry Clay and a new political party, the Whigs. Daniel Webster was also a Whig, and for the first time these three men found themselves on the same side. It was an odd combination, and it did not last long.

Henry Clay still believed in his American System. He wanted a network of roads and canals to help link different states. He believed in the need for tariffs to help industry grow in the United States. The American System had pleased the Western states, which needed roads built, and the Northern states, which needed protective tariffs.

Henry Clay represented the West, and Daniel Webster represented the North. They could work well together in the Whig party. The American System created an alliance between these two regions. Together, the North and West could control a majority of the United States.

But John Calhoun, representing the South, felt uncomfortable. The Southern states were left out of the North-West alliance. They wanted the tariffs ended.

The remedy, Calhoun decided, was to halt the growing power of the federal government. He began to push states' rights over federal power.

In doing so, Calhoun broke with the Whig party. He returned to the Democratic party, supporting the candidacy of Martin Van Buren. Martin Van Buren had nearly destroyed Calhoun's career only a few years earlier. But Van Buren was committed to states' rights, and Calhoun put aside his personal feelings. He felt that the issue of states' rights was more important than party affiliation.

In 1840, Van Buren's term as president came to an end. William Henry Harrison, a hero from the War of 1812, was the Whig candidate. He won the presidency. Unfortunately, he died after serving only one month. This was the first time in United States history that a president had died while in office. The vice-president, John Tyler, became the new president.

On a winter day in 1843, President John Tyler went on a short cruise down the Potomac in a new warship, the U.S.S. *Princeton.* Secretary of State Abel P. Upshur and Secretary of the Navy Thomas Gilmer were also on board. Among the other guests were prominent Washingtonian David Gardiner and his daughter, Julia.

Suddenly the calm of the afternoon was shattered. The "Peacemaker," one of the ship's guns, exploded. President Tyler was thrown to the deck by the blast but was not seriously hurt. Others were not so lucky. Secretary Upshur, Secretary Gilmer, and David Gardiner were killed instantly. When Julia Gardiner learned of her father's death, she fainted in the arms of the president. A few months later, she became his wife, making President Tyler the first president to be married while in office.

President Tyler had the unhappy duty of replacing the cabinet members who had died in the explosion. He chose John C. Calhoun to replace Secretary of State Upshur.

After a short hesitation, Calhoun accepted. One of Tyler's primary concerns was the annexation of Texas. Calhoun was very interested in the issue. He saw it as important to the future of the country—especially the South.

Before the 1800s, the westernmost boundary of the United States was the Mississippi River. The northern boundary was drawn along the 49th parallel, through the middle of the Great Lakes.

Then, in 1803, Thomas Jefferson bought the Louisiana Territory from France. This one purchase doubled the size of the United States' territory. With Jackson's campaign in Florida, the borders were pushed south. The entire Florida peninsula was added to the United States, along with New Orleans.

The country was still growing. When Lewis and Clark explored the Louisiana Territory, they reported an abundance of beaver, from which fur pelts could be made. Fur trappers traveled the territory, catching the beaver and selling them. The beaver pelts were needed to make top hats, which had become fashionable in Europe. The fur trappers made very good money. They also nearly caused the extinction of the beaver in the process. And they angered the Native Americans, who also caught and sold beaver pelts.

But the fur trappers mapped out the wilderness thoroughly. One group of trappers stumbled upon a passage through the Rocky Mountains. They called this passage the South Pass. The trappers told stories about their adventures and the wonderful sights they had seen. Their descriptions of the land tempted people. There were reports of fertile farmland and golden hills in California, and shining mountains in Oregon. The rest of the country began to feel crowded. People wanted to settle in the new territories. These people became pioneers and traveled to the new territories in long trains of covered wagons.

By the 1840s, the beaver had almost disappeared, and the former fur trappers took on a new role. They guided the wagon trains across the prairies and through the South Pass. From there, a southern trail led to California. Some pioneers chose to take this trail.

Another trail led to the Oregon Territory. The wagon trains would travel north to the Columbia River. Once there, the pioneers would build rafts and float down the Columbia to the Willamette Valley.

Another area that people were settling was Texas. Texas had originally been claimed by both France and Spain, but after Mexico gained its independence in 1820, it was considered part of that country. In 1821 and 1822, Stephen Austin led a group of 300 families from the United States to Texas. They started a colony.

More families joined them. By 1835, there were 35,000 settlers from the United States in Texas. That year, General Antonio López de Santa Anna overthrew the constitutional government of Mexico and became dictator. The colonies in Texas revolted against him. At first, the colonists lost many battles against Santa Anna. But they kept fighting, and finally they won their independence. Texas became a republic.

The territory of Texas was huge, comparable in size to the Louisiana Territory. The United States wanted to annex Texas—to make it a part of the country. In 1843, Texas was to join the United States.

"Annexing Texas," wrote newspaper editor John L. O'Sullivan, would be "the fulfillment of our manifest destiny to overspread the continent." The words "manifest destiny" became a catch-phrase to describe the feeling that made people leave their homes and settle in Texas, Oregon, and California.

Britain was interested in Texas, too. Britain offered to help negotiations between Texas and Mexico to settle border disputes.

John C. Calhoun watched with alarm Britain's efforts to help Texas. Britain had recently abolished slavery. Calhoun believed that Britain was trying to draw Texas into the British Empire. If it did that, they would certainly abolish slavery in the region.

If the British abolished slavery in Texas, Calhoun feared the institution would be doomed in the United States. With an antislavery country to the West, and the abolitionist movement gaining power in the North, the Southern states would be under attack from two sides. Calhoun thought he knew why the British were so interested in Texas. India, a British colony, produced cotton, like the Southern states. But Indian cotton was more expensive, since India did not allow slavery. Britain wanted to abolish slavery in the United States to drive up the price of cotton. That way, the Indian cotton could compete with the United States product.

Before the *Princeton* explosion, Calhoun had written to Secretary of State Upshur, warning him about the British. Upshur had agreed with Calhoun's conclusions. That was why John Tyler had thought of John Calhoun to replace Upshur in the State Department.

Calhoun accepted the post grudgingly. He wrote to the president, "But as nothing short of the magnitude of the crisis occasioned by the pending negotiations, could induce me to leave my retirement, I accept on the condition, that when they are concluded, I shall be at liberty to retire."

As Calhoun arrived in Washington, he found the negotiations with the Republic of Texas nearly completed. A secret treaty was signed by representatives of both governments only a week after he arrived, agreeing to the terms under which Texas would be admitted to the Union. All that remained was for the Texas government and the United States Senate to ratify the agreement.

Calhoun wanted Texas added to the Union. In the years since the Missouri Compromise, the fight over slavery had spread like a brushfire. The abolitionists were clamoring to end slavery. The South was trying to expand the institution. Texas would increase the power of the slaveholding states. As many as five states could be carved out of the territory, all slaveholding.

But Calhoun overreached himself. He used Texas to argue the merits of slavery with the new British minister, Richard Pakenham. He said his purpose was "to bring our cause...fully and favorably before the world." Using very selective census statistics, Calhoun attempted to prove that when African Americans were freed, they became prone to both mental and physical diseases.

Calhoun no longer based his defense of slavery on economic necessity. He did not attempt to downplay slavery as a temporary institution. Instead, he began to base his argument on the racist assumption that the African Americans were inferior to the other races. "The abolition of slavery," he concluded, "would (if it did not destroy the inferior [race] by conflict to which it would lead) reduce it to extremes of vice and wretchedness."

Pakenham refused to discuss Texas in these terms, which he considered extremely offensive. He had no desire to become caught up in John Calhoun's political manipulations. He did not dignify Calhoun's arguments with a reply. Instead, he pointed out that proslavery arguments and the health of freed African Americans had no bearing on whether Britain supported the Republic of Texas.

Calhoun's approach to the Oregon Territory was quite different. In contrast to his views about Texas, Calhoun urged patience on what had come to be known as the Oregon Question.

The Oregon Question had to do with the northern boundary of the United States. Britain and the United States both occupied the area. Some people wanted to annex the territory immediately to the United States, drawing the northern boundary at the 54° 40′ parallel. Their slogan was "Fifty-four forty or fight!" The British wanted to set the boundary at the Columbia River.

Calhoun thought the boundary would best be set at the 49th parallel. He argued against provoking a war with Britain over the issue. The pioneers were flooding into the territory. Each United States citizen who settled in the territory made the U.S. claim to the area more powerful.

Calhoun's decision to wait was wise. As the years passed, the number of United States citizens in the territory grew. In time, the territory became part of the United States, without provoking Britain. The northern boundary was eventually set at the 49th parallel, just as Calhoun had predicted.

But Calhoun's strategy with Texas backfired. Using Texas to promote slavery angered many people. Some senators had wanted to add Texas to the United States because it would expand the country. These senators began to think again. They were not so sure they wanted the new territory, if all it did was increase the power of the slave states. The furor over Calhoun's stance delayed the annexation for months. Calhoun lost the chance to add Texas to the Union before the next presidential election.

In 1844, James K. Polk was elected president. During his administration, Texas was finally added to the Union as a slave state. Eventually, it joined the other slave states in seceding from the United States.

Calhoun supported Polk. He expected to be kept on as secretary of state. But Calhoun had offended too many people on the Texas issue. He was dangerous to the new administration. Polk offered Calhoun a position as minister to Great Britain. This would allow Calhoun to continue his negotiations over Texas and Oregon. But what was more important, it would keep Calhoun out of the country.

John Calhoun did not want the position. He was insulted by the offer and returned home to South Carolina. He tried running for the presidency, but that soon came to nothing. Within a year, John Calhoun was back in the Senate.

Calhoun, by using Texas as an issue to promote slavery, had delayed the annexation, offended people, and deepened the gap between slave and free states. He had ruined his chances to stay on in the State Department or become president in 1848. But Calhoun hardly cared. He was committed to slavery. Everything else was secondary.

INVENTIONS AND PROGRESS

"I am beginning to believe that the culture of cotton is incompatible with any improvement which renders a country attractive to the eye...."

ANDREW PICKENS CALHOUN

Through all his years in public service, John C. Calhoun still thought of himself as a farmer. He loved the times when he could stay at his plantation, and under his care it flourished. It had been more than 30 years since he had married Floride. Their children were grown.

Anna Maria, his eldest daughter, was married. Anna Maria was always Calhoun's favorite child. From the time she was 14, in 1831, she and her father had written to each other on a regular basis. Anna Maria supplied Calhoun with vivid descriptions of the plantation, which he treasured. "Were it not for you," he once wrote, "I would not have heard a word about the Hum[m]ing birds, their familiarity, the vines, their blooms, the freshness of the spring, the green yard, the children's gardens, and finally Patrick's mechanical genius and his batteaux [boats]."

She also took an interest in politics, reading the *Register of Debates* and the *Congressional Globe*. When she was old enough, she joined her father in Washington, acting as a companion and hostess. It was in Washington that she met Thomas Clemson, who later founded Clemson College. They married in 1838.

Calhoun's second son, Patrick, was in the army and stationed at a frontier post in the Southwest. Calhoun's third son, John, was studying medicine at the University of Virginia. John Calhoun worried constantly about his namesake's health, which was delicate. His second daughter, Cornelia, was even less healthy. She suffered from a childhood spine injury and had spent years going from doctor to doctor. With the help of braces, she was finally able to achieve some mobility.

John Calhoun's youngest sons, James Edward and William Lowndes Calhoun, were both in school, but Andrew Pickens, the oldest, was now in his thirties.

Andrew Calhoun had gone to Yale, like his father, but had left without graduating. For awhile he drifted, unable to decide on a profession. But a last he had bought a plantation in Alabama. John Calhoun visited it. He was delighted. He declared the 620 acres "all prime, cleared, of which nearly 400 are in cotton, which, barring accidents, ought to make 400 pounds of clean cotton to the acre."

Cotton was now without question the primary crop in the South. It was used to make cloth. Before the beginning of the 19th century, this cloth was made by hand or on a simple loom. Factories were almost unknown in the United States. The British had factories, but they tried to keep the new technology to themselves. They wanted to control the fabric industry. They would buy raw cotton from the Southern planters, but they wanted to keep the United States from learning how to make cloth on a large scale.

In 1789, Samuel Slater arrived in the United States. He had visited many factories in Britain and had made notes on the things he saw. When he returned to the United States, he set up his own factories. Even so, American industry had no improvements British mills did not already have. But this was about to change.

In 1793, Eli Whitney invented the cotton gin, a machine that picked the seeds out of cotton bolls. Before Whitney's invention, seeds had to be picked out by hand, as John Calhoun and his brother had done when they were little. This task was difficult and time-consuming.

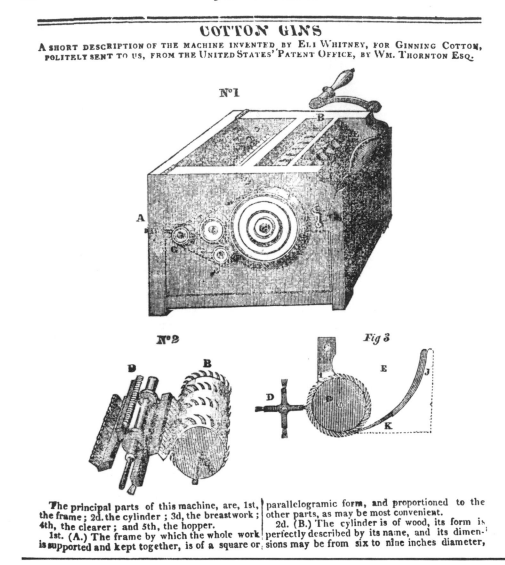

COTTON GINS

A SHORT DESCRIPTION OF THE MACHINE INVENTED BY ELI WHITNEY, FOR GINNING COTTON, POLITELY SENT TO US, FROM THE UNITED STATES' PATENT OFFICE, BY WM. THORNTON ESQ.

N°1

N°2   Fig 3

The principal parts of this machine, are, 1st, the frame; 2d. the cylinder; 3d, the breastwork; 4th, the clearer; and 5th, the hopper.

1st. (A.) The frame by which the whole work is supported and kept together, is of a square or parallelogramic form, and proportioned to the other parts, as may be most convenient.

2d. (B.) The cylinder is of wood, its form is perfectly described by its name, and its dimensions may be from six to nine inches diameter,

The cotton gin revolutionized the South's cotton industry by freeing up valuable slaves for field work.

With the invention of the cotton gin, growing cotton became much easier. One man with a cotton gin could pick as many seeds as 50 men working with just their hands. Plantation owners could use most of their slaves to grow the cotton and harvest it, rather than have the slaves laboriously pick cotton seeds. The result was a boom in cotton production, because now that cotton could be processed so quickly, it made more sense to harvest more of it. This created a still greater demand for slaves.

Two other inventions, the flying shuttle and the spinning jenny, made it much easier to manufacture cloth. Cloth became cheaper to produce, and the demand for clothing grew. As production grew, the need for cotton increased. Soon cotton was so important to the South that people called it "King Cotton."

King Cotton was not a generous ruler. In order to grow their crops, the plantation owners needed money. There were not many banks in the South, so the planters had to apply to Northern banks. These banks insisted that the planters grow cotton, because cotton seemed like a safe investment.

So the planters did. But with so many people growing cotton, the supply was greater than the demand. The prices stayed low. To make a profit, the planters had to grow more and more cotton. Small farms were unable to grow enough to make a good profit. The larger plantations became more powerful.

One way to make a good profit when cotton prices were low was to use as much slave labor as possible. By the mid–19th century, some plantations had as many as 500 slaves. In 1790, there were 700,000 slaves in the United States. In 1820, there were 2 million. By 1860, that number had doubled.

There was another problem that no one fully understood at the time. Cotton plants rob the soil of valuable nutrients. After years of growing cotton, the land became poorer and poorer. Crops got smaller. This meant that planters had to work harder to get the same amount of cotton out of the land. More and more land had to be devoted to cotton.

Andrew Calhoun had his doubts about cotton production. He wrote to his father, "The cultivation of cotton requires such incessant application to business that neither the planter, or his slave, has time to attend to anything else." He noted the bad effect that cotton had on the quality of the soil and went on to predict that the crop would eventually ruin the South.

To finance the plantation, Andrew Calhoun had borrowed money from his brother-in-law, Thomas Clemson. Even with the success of the plantation, he had trouble meeting his payments.

By the fall of 1843, Clemson could not wait any longer for his money. He threatened to sue Andrew. John Calhoun pleaded with him. But Clemson needed the money, because he had just bought his own plantation.

Calhoun decided to settle the debt himself. He borrowed some money from a friend, and some more from a bank. He had to mortgage his home, Fort Hill. He also had to pledge the money from the next cotton harvest, as well as from Andrew's crops, just to pay the interest.

Like countless other planters in the South, John Calhoun and his son were caught in a trap. The upkeep of plantations, and the need to pull more and more cotton out of the ground, kept them constantly in debt. But the more cotton that was grown, the larger the supply and the lower the price. The lower the price of cotton, the less likely they were to be able to pay their debts. "Be too proud to sacrifice your independence," he once wistfully advised Patrick Calhoun, "and to preserve it resolve to live within your means and never owe a cent of debt."

Calhoun was upset at the break between his son and his son-in-law. He was also concerned about Anna Maria. She was pregnant and was having a difficult time. Her husband was traveling much of the time, from his plantation, to a mine John Calhoun owned in Georgia, to another mine in Cuba. Anna Maria often traveled with him.

At least traveling was easier now than it had been. In 1807, Silas Whitney had built a railroad in Boston. This was before any practical steam engines had arrived in the United States. The cars on the railroad were drawn by horses.

In 1829, the first British steam locomotive, the *Stourbridge Lion*, had made its trial run in the United States. When the locomotive hissed down the track, people were amazed. It was traveling at 10 miles an hour! The next year, a race was held between the *Tom Thumb*, a locomotive built by Peter Cooper, and a horse. The *Tom Thumb* used coal for fuel. The horse won, but only because the engine broke during the race.

In 1830, the first few miles of railroad track were laid between Baltimore and Ohio. Track was also laid in South Carolina. An engine named *Best Friend of Charleston* began operating on the track. It was the first successful locomotive in the United States.

People began to see the railroads as a practical and fast way to get around. The next year, the first railway mail service in the United States started out of Charleston.

The United States fell in love with the locomotive. Cities and towns were much farther apart in the United States than in Europe. Railroads were the perfect way of joining widely separated places. People, things, even news could travel faster than ever before. By 1838, only nine years after the first steam locomotive arrived, there were 350 engines in the country, and 1,500 miles of railroad track had been laid.

Calhoun was very interested in the railroads. Years earlier, when the Erie Canal was built in New York, he had been envious. The South needed good transportation routes. He had never stopped trying to get federal funds to build roads and canals in the South. But the railroad was even better. The railroad could carry produce quickly.

Calhoun worked on a plan to build a railroad between Charleston, South Carolina, and Cincinnati, Ohio. The West would provide a market for cotton. The South would buy the produce from the West. With this exchange, John Calhoun hoped to break the alliance between the North and West and return the South to its former prominence. The problem, as Calhoun saw it, was that there were no easy trade routes between the West and South. The railroad would change all that. The railroad would join the West and the South.

But for all Calhoun's work, the North outstripped the South in building railroads. By 1860, 72 percent of the railroad track in the United States was in the Northern and Western parts of the country. This gave the Union a great advantage in the Civil War, the first war in which railroads played a significant role.

In 1843, another invention took advantage of the railroad lines. Congress budgeted $30,000 to test the telegraph. The first line was strung between Washington, D.C., and Baltimore, Maryland. On May 24, 1844, the first message was sent between the two cities. Samuel Morse, surrounded by a crowd of spectators, tapped out the words "What hath God wrought." After a few minutes, the telegraph started clicking. Morse's assistant, Alfred Vail, was sending a reply from Baltimore. What previously would have taken hours now took just minutes.

The telegraph and the railroad fulfilled John Calhoun's dream from years before. "Let us conquer space," Calhoun had urged Congress in 1817. The railroad and the telegraph were conquering both space and time. News could now travel faster than ever. Calhoun described the telegraph as "the transmission of thought by lightning itself. Magic wires," he said, "are stretching themselves in all directions over the earth, and when their mystic meshes shall have been united... our globe itself will become endowed with sensitiveness—so that whatever touches on any point, will be instantly felt on any other."

By 1861, a telegraph line stretched from California to Washington, D.C. The first message on this line was from the chief justice of California, Stephen J. Field, to President Abraham Lincoln. It was a declaration of California's loyalty to the Union.

Another invention that fascinated John Calhoun was photography. In 1849, as he was sitting in Congress, he received a message from his daughter Anna Maria. Would he come and visit her for a few weeks? When Calhoun got to New York, Anna Maria asked him to sit for the photographer Mathew Brady. She wanted a picture of her father to keep in her locket.

Photography was in its infancy. But Mathew Brady was the leading photographer in the country. Brady had already photographed many great statesmen, including Henry Clay and Daniel Webster. John Calhoun walked into the studio with his daughter and presented himself to Brady.

In 1849, it took several minutes to take a photograph. Portrait studios had special chairs with braces to keep people's heads straight. Anna Maria sat her father down in the chair. She brushed his long white hair back and arranged the drapes of his cloak around his shoulders. Brady was struck by the depth and intensity of John Calhoun's eyes. They "almost hypnotized me," he said.

John Calhoun's photograph fits the description of him given by Harriet Martineau: "The cast-iron man, who looks as if he had never been born and never could be extinguished."

John C. Calhoun, shown here in a portrait taken by the famed Civil War photographer Mathew B. Brady.

The many inventions of the past hundred years had changed the world. The advances in cloth making had created the cotton industry. They changed the South forever from a region of small, independent farms to one of large, sprawling plantations devoted entirely to cotton growing. The railroad and the telegraph sped up travel and communication between communities.

But these inventions did not come without drawbacks. The cotton industry turned slavery from a temporary measure into an institution. Calhoun had always insisted that better transportation and communication would help the United States in time of war. The Civil War would prove his foresight, but the advantage would all be on the other side. Most of the railroads and telegraph lines were in the North.

15

THE COMPROMISE OF 1850

"The South—the poor South! God knows what
will become of her!"

JOHN C. CALHOUN

n 1846, President Polk asked Congress for money to
negotiate territory disputes with Mexico. The money was
granted, but in the House, Representative David Wilmot
tried to add an amendment to the grant. This amendment, known
as the Wilmot Proviso, would prohibit the extension of slavery into
territories acquired from Mexico. The amendment was voted
down. But each time a new bill came up that dealt with the
territories, someone would try to add the Wilmot Proviso to it.
The free states' attacks were getting stronger.

In 1850, John Calhoun was joined in the Senate by both Daniel
Webster and Henry Clay. John Calhoun was old now. He was in his
sixties, but seemed at least 10 years older. His skin had paled to the
whiteness of a ghost, and his eyes burned with the intensity of coal
embers. His hair, wild and unruly, stuck out from his head, giving
the impression that he walked in a continual windstorm.

The question that came before the Senate concerned California.
California wanted to skip the territorial stage completely and had
already worked out its state constitution. The constitution pro-
hibited slavery within California's borders. It would join the United

States as a free state. After the Missouri Compromise, the slave states had complained that the government, by limiting slavery, interfered with their rights as states. Now, in the case of California, the situation was reversed. The slave states wanted to deny California the right to bar slavery within its borders.

As usual, Henry Clay had a compromise to offer. On February 5, 1850, he rose in the Senate, a stack of bills clutched in his hand. These bills, taken together, would "propose an amicable arrangement of all questions in controversy between the free and slave states, growing out of the subject of slavery."

The first bill admitted California with no restrictions on slavery. The second granted New Mexico and Utah the same freedom in writing their state constitutions. These measures both negated the Missouri Compromise, but they also would keep the hated Wilmot Proviso from being attached to the states. Clay offered a measure that would bar the slave trade from the nation's capital, but would prevent Congress from prohibiting slavery itself in the area. Clay also offered measures that would strengthen slavery. The first would create a more effective law forcing fugitive slaves to be returned to their masters. The second prevented Congress from interfering with slave trade between slave states.

Clay was attacked by all sides for this compromise. The New England states accused him of selling out to the South. The Southerners said he was failing in his duty as a senator from a slave state.

"I know no South, no North, no East, no West, to which I owe my allegiance," Clay replied. "My allegiance is the American Union and to my own State."

The alternative to the compromise was frightening. In Nashville, Tennessee, a convention was called. Delegates from nine Southern states met. Like the Hartford Convention during the War of 1812, this convention looked as if it might lead to secession.

In years past, Calhoun might have accepted the compromise. But no more. The South had given in to the needs of the North too many times. The tariffs had been oppressive, but the South had lived with tariffs in the interest of unity. But attacks on the very basis of the Southern economy, slavery, could not be borne.

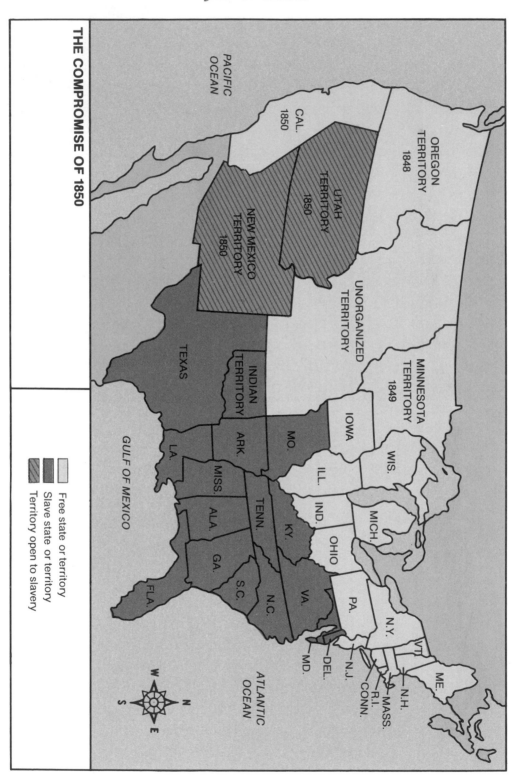

THE COMPROMISE OF 1850

PACIFIC OCEAN

CAL. 1850

OREGON TERRITORY 1848

UTAH TERRITORY 1850

NEW MEXICO TERRITORY 1850

UNORGANIZED TERRITORY

MINNESOTA TERRITORY 1849

TEXAS

INDIAN TERRITORY

ARK.

MO.

IOWA

WIS.

LA.

MISS.

ALA.

TENN.

KY.

ILL.

IND.

MICH.

OHIO

PA.

N.Y.

GA.

S.C.

N.C.

VA.

FLA.

GULF OF MEXICO

MD.

DEL.

N.J.

CONN.

R.I.

MASS.

N.H.

VT.

ME.

ATLANTIC OCEAN

Free state or territory
Slave state or territory
Territory open to slavery

N E S W

On March 4, 1850, Calhoun was tired and ill. He did not have the strength to speak. Instead, he huddled in his seat, wrapped in a black cloak, eyes burning intently out into space as Senator James M. Mason read his reply to Henry Clay. The Senate chamber hushed expectantly.

"How can the Union be preserved?" Mason began. That was an important question. Calhoun's speech continued, but first, another question had to be asked. "How has the Union been endangered?"

The danger, according to Calhoun's speech, came from the growing Northern power. At the time the Constitution was drafted, the sections, by which Calhoun meant the North and the South, were equal in power. But the Northern states had deliberately chiseled away at the South's power. By keeping slavery out of the territories, the North had kept the South from using those lands. The tariffs pulled money from the South and gave it to the North.

Strengthening the federal government, at the expense of the states, had robbed the South of the power to resist these measures. Congress decided what the extent of its power was in the nation, and then gave itself the right to use force to maintain its power. "What limitation can possibly be placed upon the powers of a government claiming and exercising such rights?" Mason read. The nature of the government had changed. It was no longer a federal republic, but a consolidated democracy, "as despotic in its tendency as any absolute Government that ever existed."

Then Calhoun's speech turned to the major issue—slavery. The North was no longer satisfied with limiting slavery, the speech said. Calhoun insisted that each slavery measure that came up was another step toward abolition, and that the South could not accept abolition because it would destroy the very basis of the Southern economy.

The speech went on to say that the responsibility to change was not the North's, not the South's. The North would have to give the South equal rights to the new territories—the right to spread slavery. The fugitive slaves who had fled to the North would have to be returned. The abolition movement would have to stop. And

Congress would have to agree to a Constitutional amendment to restore the equal powers of each region. Only then could the Union be preserved.

Clay should have been upset by Calhoun's rejection of the compromise. But both he and Webster congratulated Calhoun on the speech. The three of them had been friends, and they had been enemies. But they had all started together in the War of 1812. They had worked together, at least briefly, on promoting nationalism after the war. They had fought during the Adams administration, and they had united during Andrew Jackson's presidency. They were more than friends. They were the last survivors from what has been called America's Silver Age of statesmanship.

"I don't like Henry Clay," John Calhoun once said. "He's a bad man, an impostor, a creator of wicked schemes. I wouldn't speak to him, but, by God, I love him."

Clay and Webster knew that Calhoun's speech was one of his best. They also knew it would be his last great speech. It was obvious to everyone that John C. Calhoun was dying.

Two days later, Daniel Webster called on John Calhoun. He would speak tomorrow on the compromise. Would Calhoun come hear his speech?

Calhoun's strength was failing. Regretfully, he told his fellow senator that he would not be able to attend. But he managed to drag himself down to the Senate after all. Unnoticed, he sat down to hear Webster speak.

Webster did not see Calhoun, but when he referred to him, Calhoun struggled to rise. But he was weak, and sat back again. The second time Webster mentioned him, he managed to announce his presence.

For a moment, Webster was startled beyond words. He reached out impulsively to Calhoun, then bowed low. He was touched that his colleague had risen from his deathbed to hear the speech.

"Mr. President," Webster stated, "I wish to speak today, not as a Massachusetts man, nor as a Northern man, but as an American, and a member of the Senate of the United States.... I speak today for the preservation of the Union...." For three hours Webster spoke.

Though he rejected the institution of slavery itself, he defended the right of the South to maintain it. Slavery had predated the Constitution. It had been a condition of the original compact between the states. The North had no right to destroy it now, nor to use the "Wilmot Proviso for the mere purpose of a taunt or reproach." He urged the return of fugitive slaves, to uphold the terms of the Constitution.

People in the South were moved by Webster's speech. They saw it as what Webster had intended it to be, a peace offering. But Calhoun, though moved by his colleague's speech, knew that the course of history had already been settled. The compromise was accepted, but compromise was no longer enough. Just days after Webster's speech, he confided to Senator Mason that the Union would soon be destroyed. "I fix its probable occurrence within twelve years or three presidential terms," he said. "You and others of your age will probably live to see it; I shall not." A few weeks later, John Calhoun died. His son John, Jr., was at his bedside.

In the years following Calhoun's death, the differences between the North and the South only got bigger. In July 1854, the Kansas-Nebraska Act made slavery legally possible in these two potential states—if the states voted for it. Proslavery and antislavery settlers poured into Kansas, each trying to get a majority in the state. The fights between these two groups gave the state the name "Bleeding Kansas."

The violence in Kansas spread bad feeling throughout the United States. The Whig party broke up. Antislavery people from that party formed a new political party—what we know today as the Republican party.

In 1857, the Supreme Court heard a case called *Dred Scott* v. *Sandford*. Dred Scott was a slave. His master took him into territory where slavery was illegal. Later, Dred Scott sued for his freedom. His argument was that he had been freed by virtue of being in a free territory. The Supreme Court ruled against Dred Scott. This decision effectively meant that Congress could not exclude slavery in the territories.

Southerners rejoiced in the decision. But the Republicans refused to accept it. Several Northern states passed "personal-liberty" laws.

THE TUMULTUOUS FIFTIES

Throughout the 1850s, the United States was torn over the issue of slavery. The question of whether Kansas should allow slave ownership divided the West between "free staters" and proslavery settlers. Violent clashes became so common that people called the territory "Bleeding Kansas." This unrest reached a climax in a single brutal week in the spring of 1856. On May 21, a group of "border ruffians" rode into Lawrence, Kansas, a free-state stronghold, pillaged the town, and killed five citizens. The following day, a proslavery senator named Preston Brooks pummelled his fellow legislator Charles Sumner with a cane on the floor of the Senate. Several days before, Sumner, known for his sharp tongue and rough manner, had given a speech denouncing "the crime against Kansas" committed by proslavery elements. Finally, two days after Sumner's beating, abolitionist John Brown and several of his sons took revenge for the sacking of Lawrence by killing five proslavery settlers near Pottawatomie Creek, hacking their victims to death with broadswords. At the decade's end, the nation was on the verge of chaos.

Chief Justice Roger B. Taney, whose famous *Dred Scott* decision of March 6, 1857 destroyed the Missouri Compromise.

Under the fugitive slave law, slaves who escaped into free territories had to be returned to their owners.

Charles Sumner (far right) never completely recovered from the beating he received from Preston "Bully" Brooks.

These laws encouraged people to disobey federal laws providing for the return of fugitive slaves.

In 1859, a man named John Brown led an attack on Harpers Ferry, Virginia. John Brown was a radical abolitionist who occasionally resorted to terrorism in his attempts to gain freedom for blacks. He planned to seize a federal arsenal and start a slave uprising. Robert E. Lee led the troops that caught John Brown. Brown was tried and hanged. He became a martyr to the cause of abolition.

In 1860, Abraham Lincoln ran for president. He supported a platform that included tariffs for manufacturers, free homesteads for farmers and workers, central banking for merchants and financiers, and government-subsidized railroads for everyone. All these programs were hated by the South, except possibly the railroads. But even worse, in 1858, Lincoln had argued against slavery in a series of debates with his rival for the presidency, Stephen A. Douglas.

Before the election, the Southern states advocated secession if Lincoln should win. Lincoln was elected in November 1860. In December, South Carolina became the first state to secede. Mississippi, Florida, Alabama, Georgia, Louisiana, and Texas soon followed.

President Lincoln stated that secession was illegal. He would hold onto federal possessions in the seceding states. On April 14, 1861, Confederate troops seized Fort Sumter in South Carolina. Lincoln called for Union troops, and the Southern states saw this as an act of war. Virginia, Arkansas, North Carolina, and Tennessee joined the Confederacy.

For all of his career, John Calhoun had tried to uphold the Union. Upholding the Union had meant standing up to Britain in the War of 1812. It had meant binding the republic together with roads, canals, and the newer inventions, the railroad and the telegraph. It had meant building up a strong military in case of war. It had meant trying to forge new methods of government, such as nullification. It had meant buckling down to oppressive tariffs. It had meant accepting compromise after painful compromise.

But John Calhoun had been unable and unwilling to make the most necessary sacrifice to keep the Union together. Underlying every other problem—the tariffs, the territorial disputes, state vs. federal powers—lay two basic issues: slavery, and the struggle between the North and the South for dominance. The roots of the Civil War reached all the way back to Hamilton and Jefferson, all the way back to the Constitution. Either side might have prevented the Civil War, but only by giving in. The failure to stop the war belonged to everyone, even to a prophet like John C. Calhoun.

Near the end of the Civil War, Walt Whitman was working in a hospital tent. He heard two soldiers talking. The first one said that he had seen a monument to John C. Calhoun in Charleston.

"I have seen Calhoun's monument," the other soldier replied. "What you saw is not the real monument. But I have seen it. It is the desolated, ruined South; nearly the whole generation of young men between seventeen and thirty destroyed or maimed; all the old families used up; the slaves unloosed and become the masters, and the name of Southerner blackened with every shame—all that is Calhoun's monument."

TIMETABLE OF EVENTS IN THE LIFE OF

JOHN C. CALHOUN

March 18, 1782	Born near Abbeville, South Carolina
1802	Begins studies at Yale
1804	Graduates from Yale
1806	Graduates from Litchfield Law School
1807	Elected to the South Carolina legislature
1810	Elected to the U.S. House of Representatives
1812	Aids in passage of the declaration of war for the War of 1812
1817	Appointed secretary of war by President James Monroe
1820	Aids in passage of the Missouri Compromise
1824	Elected as John Quincy Adam's vice-president
1828	Elected as Andrew Jackson's vice-president Writes *Exposition and Protest*
1832	Resigns as vice-president
1844	Appointed secretary of state
March 31, 1850	Dies in Washington, D.C.

SUGGESTED READING

Asimov, Isaac. *Our Federal Union: The United States from 1816 to 1865*. Boston: Houghton Mifflin, 1975.

Crane, William D. *Patriotic Rebel: John C. Calhoun*. New York: Julian Messner, 1972.

Goodman, Walter. *Black Bondage: The Life of Slaves in the South*. New York: Farrar, Straus & Giroux, 1969.

Greenblatt, Miriam. *John Quincy Adams: Sixth President of the United States*. Ada, Ok.: Garrett Education Corp., 1988.

Hayman, LeRoy. *The Road to Fort Sumter*. New York: Crowell, 1972.

Kelly, Rgina Z. *Henry Clay*. Boston: Houghton Mifflin, 1960.

Marrin, Albert. *1812, the War Nobody Won*. New York: Atheneum, 1985.

Marsh, Carole. *Out of the Mouths of Slaves*. Bath, N.C.: Gallopade Publishing Group, 1989.

Morris, Richard B. *The Founding of the Republic*. Minneapolis: Lerner, 1985.

Sabin, Leo. *Andrew Jackson, Frontier Patriot*. Mahwah, N.J.: Troll, 1985.

Wilkie, Katherine E. *The Man Who Wouldn't Give Up: Henry Clay*. New York: Julian Messner, 1961.

SELECTED SOURCES

Aptheker, Herbert. *Nat Turner's Slave Rebellion*. New York: Washington Square Press, 1966.

Capers, Gerald M. *John C. Calhoun—Opportunist: A reappraisal*. Gainesville: University of Florida Press, 1960.

Coit, Margaret L. *John C. Calhoun: American Portrait*. Boston: Houghton Mifflin, 1950.

Collins, Bruce. *The Origins of the American Civil War*. New York: Holmes and Meier, 1981.

Freehling, William W., ed. *The Nullification Era: A Documentary Record*. New York: Harper & Row, 1967.

Hofstadter, Richard. "John C. Calhoun: The Marx of the Master Class," *The American Political Tradition & the Men Who Made It*. New York: Washington Square Press, 1974.

Johnson, Gerald W. *America's Silver Age: The Statecraft of Clay-Webster-Calhoun*. New York and London: Harper and Bros., 1939.

Koch, Adrienne, and Peden, William, eds. *The Selected Writings of John and John Quincy Adams*. New York: Knopf, 1946.

Linton, Calvin D., ed. *The Bicentennial Almanac*. Nashville: Thomas Nelson, 1975.

Meriwether, Robert, ed. *The Calhoun Papers*, Vols I-V. Columbia: University of South Carolina Press, 1959–1986.

Morison, Samuel Eliot. *The Oxford History of the American People*, Volume Two 1789–1877. New York and Scarborough: Oxford, 1972.

Niven, John. *John C. Calhoun and the Price of Union: A Biography*. Baton Rouge: Louisiana State University Press, 1988.

Peterson, Merrill D. *The Great Triumvirate: Webster, Clay and Calhoun*. New York, Oxford, University Press, 1987.

Stephenson, Wendell Holmes. *A Basic History of the Old South*. Princeton: Van Nostrand, 1959.

Trevor I. Williams. *The History of Invention: From Stone Axes to Silicon Chips*. New York: Facts on File, 1987.

Wiltse, Charles M. *John C. Calhoun: Nationalist, 1872–1828*. Indianapolis and New York: Russell and Russell, 1944.

Wiltse, Charles M. *John C. Calhoun: Nullifier, 1829–1839*. Indianapolis and New York: Russell and Russell, 1949.

Wiltse, Charles M. *John C. Calhoun: Sectionalist, 1840–1850*. Indianapolis and New York: Russell and Russell, 1951.

INDEX

Abolitionists, 98, 101–2, 126
Adams, John Quincy
 and abolitionist movement, 102
 and Eaton affair, 86–87
 and election of 1824, 75–78, 84
 and election of 1828, 83
 as president, 78–80
 as secretary of state, 61, 64–65
 and slavery, 100–102
 and Treaty of Ghent, 45–46
Alabama
 cotton production, 55
 secedes, 126
 and treaty with Creeks, 51
Alien Act (1799), 29–30
Ambrister, Robert, 64, 65
American Colonization Society, 98
American System, 56–58, 60, 94, 103
Antislavery movement, 98
Arbuthnot, Alexander, 64, 65
Arkansas, secession of, 126
Articles of Confederation, 16
Austin, Stephen, 106

Bank bill, 49, 57–60
Bank of the United States, 49, 57
Barron, James, 31
Berlin Decree, 32, 43
Bill of Rights, 18, 60
Bleeding Kansas, 123
Brady, Mathew, 116
Brook, Sir Isaac, 41
Brown, John, 126
Butler, William, 42

Calhoun, Andrew Pickens (son), 35,
 111, 113–14
Calhoun, Anna Maria (Clemson)
 (daughter), 110, 114, 116
Calhoun, Cornelia (daughter), 99, 111
Calhoun, Elizabeth (daughter), 69
Calhoun, Floride (daughter), 54
Calhoun, Floride Colhoun (wife),
 34–35, 55, 61–62, 68–69, 81,
 85–86, 99–100, 110
Calhoun, James (brother), 20, 25
Calhoun, James Edward (son), 111

Calhoun, John C., 15
  and annexation of Texas, 104, 106–9
  born, 15
  and Compromise of 1850, 118–23
  in Congress, 33–34, 41–45, 48–49
  and currency committee, 57
  dies, 123
  early years, 13, 18–21
  and Eaton affair, 85–87
  education, 19–20, 25–27, 29
  and election of 1824, 76–78
  and election of 1828, 82–83
  as farmer, 13, 18–21
  and Force Bill, 93
  in foreign relations committee,
    37–40
  and Jackson, 81–87
  in law office in Charleston, 28
  at Litchfield Law School, 29
  marries Floride Colhoun, 34
  and military academy, 66–67
  and Missouri question, 74
  and national bank, 59–60
  and nullification, 88–95
  and Oregon Question, 108–9
  as secretary of state, 104, 107
  as secretary of war, 61–66
  and slavery, 99–102
  in state legislature, 33–34
  as vice-president, 78–81
  and War of 1812, 40–45
  and Whigs, 103–4
  at Yale, 25–27
Calhoun, John, Jr. (son), 81, 111, 123
Calhoun, Martha Caldwell (mother),
  15, 20, 25
Calhoun, Patrick (brother), 19, 29
Calhoun, Patrick (father), 13–15, 19, 20
Calhoun, Patrick (son), 111, 114
Calhoun, William (brother), 20, 61
Calhoun, William Lowndes (son), 86,
  111
California, 105
  statehood, 118–19

Canada, and War of 1812, 41
Chesapeake, U.S.S. (frigate), 31–32, 45
Civil War, 127
Clay, Henry, 87, 116
  and American System, 56–57
  and Compromise of 1850, 118–23
  and election of 1824, 75–78
  and Missouri Compromise, 70–74
  and nullification, 94–95
  and protective tariff, 58–59
  as secretary of state, 78
  as Speaker of the House, 35–37, 43,
    56, 70–72
  and Whigs, 103
Clayton, John Middleton, 94
Clemson, Anna Maria Calhoun
  (daughter), 110, 114, 116
Clemson, Thomas, 110, 113–14
Clermont (steamboat), 56
Cobb, Jeremiah, 98
Cockburn, Sir George, 47
Colhoun, Floride (mother-in-law),
  27–28, 29, 34, 54
Colhoun, Floride (the younger), 27–28,
  34. *See also* Calhoun, Floride
Colhoun, James Edward, 28, 34
Colhoun, John (cousin), 27
Colhoun, John Ewing, 27–28, 34
Colhoun, Joseph, 33
Compromise of 1850, 118–23
Congress, 17, 35
  and election of 1824, 77–78
Connecticut, and Hartford
  Convention, 50
Constitution, 17–19, 59–60
  Bill of Rights, 18, 60
  First Amendment, 30
Constitution, U.S.S., (ship), 41
Constitutional Convention, 16
Continental Congress, 16
Cooper, Peter, 114
Cornwallis, Sir Charles, 15
Cotton, 16, 19, 55, 111–13
Cotton gin, 111–12

Crawford, William, 65, 75–77, 79, 82, 86, 87
Cumming, William, 77

Dallas, George M., 49
Davis, Jefferson, 66, 67
Declaration of Independence, 18
Democratic party, 80, 82
Detroit, captured by British, 41
Direct tax, 58
District of 96, 14
Douglas, Stephen A., 126
Draft, 63
Dred Scott v. *Sandford*, 123
Dwight, Timothy, 27, 30

Eaton, John, 85–87
Eaton, Margaret O'Neill (Peggy), 85-87
Election
    of 1800, 30
    of 1824, 75–79, 84
    of 1828, 82–83
    of 1840, 104
    of 1844, 109
    of 1860, 126
Embargo, 32–33, 42
Embargo Act (1807), 32
Erie Canal, 115
Exposition and Protest (Calhoun), 90, 92

Federalists, 24, 27, 30, 41–52
Felder, John, 26–27, 29
Field, Stephen J., 116
First Amendment, 30
Fishing rights, 51–52
Florida
    Pensacola captured, 51, 63–64
    secession of, 126
    statehood, 105
Force Bill, 93
Fort Dearborn, 41
"Fort Hill Address" (Calhoun), 92
Fort Sumter, 126

France, war with Great Britain, 32–33
French Revolution, 24

Gag rule, 102
Gardiner, David, 104
Garrison, William Lloyd, 98
Georgia, secession of, 126
Ghent, Treaty of, 45–46, 51–52
Gilmer, Thomas, 104
Great Britain
    and *Chesapeake* incident, 31–32
    embargo, 32–33
    and Oregon Question, 108
    and Texas, 106–7
    and War of 1812, 40–46
    war with France, 32–33
Guerriere (frigate), 41

Hamilton, Alexander, 22, 24, 48, 50
Harpers Ferry, 126
Harrison, William Henry, 104
Hartford Convention, 50, 52
Hayne, Robert Y., 90, 93
Hopkins, Samuel, 41
House foreign relations committee, 37–38, 40
House Ways and Means Committee, 57
Hull, Henry, 41
Hull, Isaac, 41

Inauguration of Jackson, 84–85
Indian affairs, 63–64
Indirect tax, 58

Jackson, Andrew, 50, 63, 81
    and Eaton affair, 85–87
    and election of 1824, 76–78
    and election of 1828, 82–83
    in Forida, 51, 63–64
    inauguration of, 84–85
    at New Orleans, 51–52
    and nullification, 90–95
    as president, 83–87
Jackson, Rachel, 83

Jay, William, 100
Jefferson, Thomas, 18, 48, 90–91
   elected president, 30
   and Embargo Act, 32–33
   and Missouri Compromise, 73–74
   and Non-Intercourse Act, 33
   as secretary of state, 22, 24
Johnston, Joseph E., 66, 67

Kansas-Nebraska Act (1854), 123
Kentucky, statehood, 70
Kentucky Resolution, 30, 90

Lawrence, James, 45
Lee, Henry (Light-horse Harry), 66
Lee, Robert E., 66, 67, 126
Leopard, H.M.S. (ship), 31
Lewis and Clark, 105
Liberator, 98
Liberia, 98
Library of Congress, 47, 48
Lincoln, Abraham, 116, 126
Litchfield Law School, 29
Livingston, Edward, 93
Long Cane Creek district, 13–14
Louisiana, secession of, 126
Louisiana Territory, 50, 105
Lowndes, William, 37, 57–58, 69, 87
   and election of 1824, 76–77

Madison, Dolley, 47, 48
Madison, James, 18, 40, 43, 45, 59–60,
   62
Maine, statehood, 70–72
Manifest destiny, 106
Manufacturing, 56, 111, 113
Marie Antoinette, Queen, 24
Martineau, Harriet, 116
Maryland, Catholics in, 16
Mason, James M., 121, 123
Massachusetts, and Hartford
   Convention, 50
McDuffie, George, 77, 81, 92
Michilimackinac, capture of, 41
Milan Decree, 32, 43
Mississippi, secession of, 126

Missouri, statehood, 69–70, 73
Missouri Compromise, 69–74, 100
Monroe, James, 59, 61, 86, 100
Morse, Samuel, 115–16

Napoleon Bonaparte, 32–33, 43–45, 78
National bank, 49, 57–60
Native Americans, 14, 63–64
   and fur trappers, 105
   and War of 1812, 41, 50–51
New England
   manufacturing in, 56
   Puritans in, 16
New Hampshire, and Hartford
   Convention, 50
New Mexico, statehood, 119
New Orleans, battle of, 51–52
New York, and Hartford Convention,
   50
Non-Importation Act, 42–43
Non-Intercourse Act (1809), 33
North Carolina, secession of, 126
Nullification, 88–95

Oneida (ship), 41
Orders in Council, 32, 38, 40, 42–43,
   45
Oregon Question, 108–9
Oregon Territory, 105, 108–9
Osborne, Selleck, 29
O'Sullivan, John L., 106

Paine, Thomas, 19
Pakenham, Richard, 107–8
Pakenham, Sir Edward, 52
Pennsylvania, Quakers in, 16
Pensacola, battle of, 51
Personal-liberty laws, 123, 126
Phipps, Benjamin, 98
Pierce, Franklin, 66
Polk, James K., 109
Princeton, U.S.S. (ship), 104
Protective tariff, 58–59
Puritans, 16

Quakers, 16
Queenston Heights, battle of, 42

Railroad, 114–16

Randolph, John, 37–39, 41, 58, 72, 80–81

Reeve, Tapping, 29, 30

Register of Debates, 110

Republicans, 24, 27, 30, 123

Revolutionary War, 15, 19

Rights of Man, The (Paine), 19

Santa Anna, Antonio Lópèz de, 106

Secession, 30, 42, 50, 52, 119, 126

Sedition Act (1799), 29–30

Slater, Samuel, 111

Slavery, 17, 100–102

  and annexation of Texas, 106-9

  and Compromise of 1850, 118–23

  and cotton, 113, 117

  and *Dred Scott* v. *Sandford*, 123

  and Kansas-Nebraska Act, 123

  and Missouri Compromise, 69–74

  and Wilmot Proviso, 118, 119

Slaves, 19

  Nat Turner's Rebellion, 96–98

  and Seminoles, 63

South Carolina

  cotton in, 55

  and Force Bill, 93

  Provincial Assembly, 14–15

  ratifies Constitution, 18

  and Revolutionary War, 19

  secedes, 126

  tariff and nullification, 89–95

Spinning jenny, 113

States' rights, 90–95, 104

Steamboat, 56

Steam locomotive, 114

Supreme Court, 123

Tariffs, 58–59, 88–95

Taxes, 58

Telegraph, 115–16

Tennessee, secedes, 126

Texas

  annexation, 104, 106–9

  becomes republic, 106

  secedes, 126

  statehood, 109

Transportation, 59, 114–116

Travis, Joseph, 96

Turner, Nat, and slave uprising, 96–98

Tyler, John, 104, 107

Tyler, Julia Gardiner, 104

Underground Railroad, 101

Upshur, Abel, P., 104, 107

Utah, statehood, 119

Vail, Alfred, 115–16

Van Buren, Martin, 79–80, 82, 86, 87, 90, 92, 104

Vermont

  and Hartford Convention, 50

  statehood, 70

Virginia, secedes, 126

Virginia Resolution, 30, 90

Voltaire, 48–49

Waddel, Catherine Calhoun (sister), 19

Waddel, Moses, 19–20, 25

Waddel Academy, 25

War Hawks, 37–39, 41, 45, 56

War Mess, 37

War of 1812, 40–48, 50–52

Washington, D.C., sacked, 47–48

Washington, George, 15, 16, 22, 30

Ways and Means Committee, 57

Webster, Daniel, 52, 90, 116

  and Compromise of 1850, 118–23

  and Force Bill, 93

  and foreign relations committee, 43–45

  and national bank, 57

  and Whigs, 103

West Point Military Academy, 66–67

Whigs, 103-4, 123

Whitman, Walt, 127

Whitney, Eli, 111

Whitney, Silas, 114

Wilmot, David, 118

Wilmot Proviso, 118–19

Yorktown, battle of, 15

Teresa Celsi lives in Portland, Oregon, where she was born in 1962. She graduated from New York University in 1985, after which she worked as a children's textbook editor. Celsi is the author of several books for children, including the biographies *Squanto and the First Thanksgiving* and *Rosa Parks and the Montgomery Bus Boycott* and the fiction work *The Fourth Little Pig*. Celsi has also founded a theater company in New York City and written a musical, *Pink Vinyl/Blue Guitar*, and a play, *El Dorado*.

PICTURE CREDITS

Library of Congress: 23, 33, 36, 44, 53, 62, 67, 79, 84, 97, 99, 117, 124, 125 (bottom). Schomburg Center for Research in Black Culture, New York Public Library, Astor, Lenox and Tilden Foundations: 125 (top). Smithsonian Institution: 112. South Carolina Historical Society: 28. U.S. Navy: 46.

Cover: Clemson University (portrait, Exposition and Protest manuscript); The Granger Collection (cotton plantation).